YOUNG MARX

Richard Bean and Clive Coleman

YOUNG MARX

OBERON BOOKS
LONDON

WWW.OBERONBOOKS.COM

First published in 2017 by Oberon Books Ltd
521 Caledonian Road, London N7 9RH
Tel: +44 (0) 20 7607 3637 / Fax: +44 (0) 20 7607 3629
e-mail: info@oberonbooks.com
www.oberonbooks.com

A catalogue record for this book is available from the British
Library.

PB ISBN: 9781786822833
E ISBN: 9781786822840

Printed and bound by 4EDGE Limited, Hockley, Essex, UK.
eBook conversion by CPI Group (UK) Ltd, Croydon, CR0 4YY.

Characters

(age in play and actual age in November 1850 if different.)

KARL MARX, 32

FRIEDRICH ENGELS, 29

JENNY VON WESTPHALEN, 36

JENNY CAROLINE 'QUI QUI' MARX, 10
(actual age, six years old)

GUIDO 'FAWKSEY' MARX, 3
(actual age, one year old)

HELENE 'NYM' DEMUTH (the maid), 30

AUGUST VON WILLICH, 39

EMMANUEL BARTHÉLEMY, 30

KONRAD SCHRAMM, 21
(actual age, twenty-eight years old)

GERT 'DOC' SCHMIDT, 32

And others, notably – SERGEANT SAVAGE, CONSTABLE CRIMP,
MRS MULLETT (Whelk seller), MR FLEECE (Pawnbroker),
MR GRABINER (Bailiff), HELMUT (Prussian spy), and émigrés,
library staff, readers, traders, Londoners…

SET

Soho 1850. Multi location, Soho streets, rented apartment
interior, Hampstead Heath, function room of Red Lion,
pawnbroker's, graveyard.

LANGUAGE/CONVENTION

When German characters are speaking to English characters
their speech is accented.

When in the company of Germans, it is not.

The presumption being, amongst their own,
they are all speaking German.

Young Marx premiered at The Bridge Theatre, London on 26 October 2017 with the following cast in order of speaking:

MR FLEECE, PAWNBROKER	Duncan Wisbey
KARL MARX	Rory Kinnear
SERGEANT SAVAGE	Joseph Wilkins
JENNY VON WESTPHALEN	Nancy Carroll
FRIEDRICH ENGELS	Oliver Chris
HELENE 'NYM' DEMUTH	Laura Elphinstone
GUIDO 'FAWKSEY' MARX	Logan Clark
	Rupert Turnbull
	Joseph Walker
GERT 'DOC' SCHMIDT	Tony Jayawardena
KONRAD SCHRAMM	Eben Figueiredo
JENNY CAROLINE 'QUI QUI' MARX	Dixie Egerickx
	Matilda Shapland
	Harriet Turnbull
MR GRABINER, BAILIFF	Scott Karim
MRS MULLETT, WHELK SELLER	Alana Ramsey
HELMUT, PRUSSIAN SPY	Fode Simbo
AUGUST VON WILLICH	Nicholas Burns
EMMANUEL BARTHÉLEMY	Miltos Yerolemou
CONSTABLE CRIMP	William Troughton
BEARDED MAN IN LIBRARY	Duncan Wisbey
MRS WHITEHEAD, LIBRARIAN	Sophie Russell
CONSTABLE SINGE	Scott Karim
PASTOR FLINT	Fode Simbo

Other parts played by members of the Company

Director	Nicholas Hytner
Designer	Mark Thompson
Lighting Designer	Mark Henderson
Music	Grant Olding
Sound Designer	Paul Arditti
Fight Director	Kate Waters
Assistant Director	Sean Linnen

Act One

SCENE ONE

(1850. A pawnbroker's. On one end of the counter, MR FLEECE is looking at paperwork. His assistant JIM is polishing a brass. MARX enters, produces the Argyll from under his coat and places it on the other end of counter.)

MR FLEECE: *(Without looking up.)* In a moment, I'm going to ask you to bring that item over here and tell me what it is.

(MARX picks up the Argyll.)

Not yet!

(FLEECE finally looks up from his papers.)

Now, bring it over here, and tell me what it is.

(MARX delivers the ARGYLL to that bit of the counter before MR FLEECE.)

MARX: Also, it's a gravy warmer, an Argyll, an original, invented by the eponymous Duke. *(Also pronounced alzo.)*

MR FLEECE: And what was he called?

MARX: Argyll.

MR FLEECE: Is that why it's called an Argyll?

MARX: Who knows?!

MR FLEECE: What's its value?

MARX: *(Beat.)* Its use value or its exchange value?

MR FLEECE: What's the difference?

MARX: How long do you have?

MR FLEECE: I've got all day mate.

MARX: That may not be enough time. To fix an exchange value we would need to know the socially necessary labour time required to produce this commodity with the average degree of skill und intensity currently prevalent.

MR FLEECE: *(Nods to JIM to leave.)* Jim!

(JIM leaves.)

MARX: Where is Jim going?

MR FLEECE: There's always something. Love, money, netting. *(Beat.)* So, is this a horse?

MARX: Nein!

MR FLEECE: Good. That means we can take a butchers at its arse.

(MR FLEECE picks up the Argyll and turns it over, to look at the hallmarks.)

Let's see how much silver they reckon we got here?

MARX: Why does that interest you? The value of any commodity is an entirely social characteristic. The contribution of the silver is chimerical, arbitrary.

(MR FLEECE puts the Argyll down.)

MR FLEECE: See what I did there? I had a look at the hallmark, put it back down. Had a look, put it down. 'cause you've made me mind up for me. Since it's entirely arbitrary, I'll give you one penny.

MARX: Is that all! It's a family heirloom.

MR FLEECE: Are you Scottish then?

MARX: Jawohl!

MR FLEECE: So what's your name then son?

MARX: Karl Heinrich Marx.

MR FLEECE: A Jew?

MARX: Yes, from a long line of rabbis, most of whom were also Jewish. It's my wife who's Scottish.

MR FLEECE: And what's your wife's name?

MARX: Frau Jenny Von Westphalen. She is the daughter of Baron Ludwig von Westphalen whose mother was Anne Wishart who was descended from the totally Scottish Earls of Argyll.

MR FLEECE: Do you expect me to believe that a penniless German Jew married into the Scottish aristocracy?

MARX: I'm not saying they were happy about it. On the wedding day, I was only invited to the reception.

MR FLEECE: In a moment, I'm going to put this Argyll on this shelf here.

MARX: Und how much –

MR FLEECE: Not yet!!

(FLEECE picks up the Argyll and puts it on the shelf.)

Do you see what I did there? I picked it up and I put on the shelf. The stolen goods shelf. 'Cause you've half inched this ain't yer?!

(Re-enter JIM with policeman.)

SGT SAVAGE: Morning Len. What we got here?

MR FLEECE: Comedian.

MARX: We've met before officer.

SGT SAVAGE: Maybe, maybe not. We policemen, we all dress the same.

MARX: Mein singular offence ist to be poor. Can you arrest me for that?

SGT SAVAGE: Dunno. Policing's new to us all.

MR FLEECE: Says this Argyll is a family heirloom.

MARX: It is my wife's inheritance!

SGT SAVAGE: Does she know you've got it?

3

MARX: Does mein wife know that I'm pawning her inheritance?! Of course not!

SGT SAVAGE: My first volunteer. I'm gonna arrest you –

(MARX runs out of the shop.)

Stop thief!

End of Scene.

SCENE TWO

(MARX runs from the pawnbroker's shop heading downstage. A police whistle sounds.)

SGT SAVAGE: *(Off.)* Stop thief! Thief!

(MARX heads upstage left but is blocked by a costermonger's cart.)

BUTCHER: Oi! Marx! You owe me!

MARX: Tomorrow!

BAKER: Grab him, he's wanted!

TOBACCONIST: I got him.

(The TOBACCONIST has grabbed him by the coat, but MARX wriggles out of the coat, leaving the coat behind as he heads back downstage. SGT SAVAGE and the PAWNBROKER run on and confront MARX, who stops in his tracks, and seeing a drainpipe, he shimmies up it.

SGT SAVAGE: Marx, you're under arrest! Come down!

TOBACCONIST: Bloody refugees!

BAKER: You'll get no more bread from me Marx!

WINE MERCHANT: He don't want your bread, he wants your bakery!

BUTCHER: Settle your bills like an Englishman.

(MARX is on the roof by now.)

TOBACCONIST: You damage my tiles I'll have you!

4

PAWNBROKER: Bloody German tea leaves!

WINE MERCHANT: You can't close a window round here without trapping a refugee's fingers.

COAL MERCHANT: Three and sixpence or no more coal, never!

(MARX falls through a skylight.)

TOBACCONIST: Oh dear, that's the end of him.

SGT SAVAGE: Where's he live?

WINE MERCHANT: Dean Street. Dunno the number.

SGT SAVAGE: D'yer have a name?

WINE MERCHANT: Monsieur Ramboz.

BAKER: No! They're German, Marx.

(The rooftop chase continues.)

MARX: It's been a pleasure! À la prochain!

SCENE THREE

(The apartment in Soho. At all times the main door is bolted on the inside. Regular visitors and residents have their own coded knock. Pen and ink portraits of the spies who follow them hang from the dado rail. Two large suitcases are open on the floor, half filled with superior dresses. There is a loud coded knock at the door – two short knocks, one long pause, two short knocks. JENNY enters from the upstage left bedroom with a dress which she drops into one of the cases. She opens the door. ENGELS enters, carrying a case, and a package.)

JENNY: General!

(She bursts into tears and throws herself into ENGELS' arms.)

ENGELS: Hey, Jenny, come on. What's all this?

JENNY: You got my letter?

ENGELS: I'm here.

JENNY: It's him, it's Moor!

5

ENGELS: Of course it's Moor. Everything's Moor.

(JENNY continues to pack.)

JENNY: I'm leaving him.

ENGELS: You can't.

JENNY: I have to go.

ENGELS: He needs you.

JENNY: What about me? What do I need!

ENGELS: Yes, very well, to hell with the man you love.

JENNY: I became a pauper, a refugee because I believed in the revolution but no family can live like this. We have nothing. There is no money, and we have no money coming. Five of us, in one room.

ENGELS: Five?

JENNY: Nym!

ENGELS: Yes. Of course.

JENNY: If I go out into the street I am assailed by our creditors. I eat once a day, with the children. We can't afford a proper doctor for Fawksey. We only have Doc Schmidt. I steal coal. Did you hear me? I steal coal.

ENGELS: I imagine you do it with great style.

JENNY: The only reason the bailiff hasn't taken these dresses is because they were in hock until an hour ago. He as good as lives here.

ENGELS: The bailiff?

JENNY: Piece by piece, item by item, I am reduced. Soon I will be nothing. We have one good chair.

(She points out the one good chair, on which ENGELS sits.)

ENGELS: Thank you. You can't leave the children.

JENNY: Fawksey has Nym, he thinks she's his mother, and Qui Qui doesn't need me, she's at school.

ENGELS: You and Moor just need to –

JENNY: – we can't *just* do anything, we don't talk.

ENGELS: Alright. What's he done?

JENNY: He's given up.

ENGELS: On what?

JENNY: Everything. Everything, except finding new levels of humiliation to subject his wife and children to. Credit where it's due, he's redoubled his efforts there. He's stopped going to League meetings.

ENGELS: He's stopped going to the League, which he runs?

JENNY: He's not writing.

ENGELS: Of course he's writing, that's what he does. He's a pedigree racehorse –

JENNY: – and I have to clean out his stall!? I've negotiated commissions for him, articles, that's money, and Meissner in Germany has signed for the book. That's what I do, that's my work, I spend every waking hour writing letters, opening doors, placating everyone he's infuriated, which is everyone! And now, this.

(She hands ENGELS a letter.)

ENGELS: What's this?

JENNY: His letter applying for a job, on the railway.

ENGELS: It only takes one intellectual to bugger up a railway.

JENNY: This is not an act of revolution!

ENGELS: He's Europe's most wanted terrorist, no one's going to put him in charge of a train. He'll never get past the interview.

JENNY: Oh he'll have an answer for everything. Do you have a criminal record? Not in Canada. What was your first job? Rejecting Feuerbach, Hegel and God. And he'd make them believe that it was railway related.

7

ENGELS: Na, he won't get an interview. They won't be able to read his handwriting. He can't read his own handwriting.

JENNY: He knows that, he's asked me to scriven for him. I refused. I can't –

ENGELS: – be the wife of a railway worker?

(A coded knock at the front door. Three knocks, beat, and one knock.)

JENNY: Nym.

(ENGELS unbolts the door. NYM enters.)

ENGELS: My dear Nym.

NYM: General.

ENGELS: The intellectual's housemaid of choice!

(ENGELS grabs her by the waist.)

NYM: Remember the ten commandments. Moses got Him down to ten but adultery's still in.

(She pushes him off.)

JENNY: Yes, General, how is Mary?

ENGELS: Mary is in rude health thank you.

NYM: And her sister, Lizzie?

ENGELS: Even ruder.

JENNY: Have you seen them since your return from Europe?

ENGELS: Weekends, you know. I can't ever live in the north again.

JENNY: Was it your life ambition to set up a love nest with two Irish sisters in a worker's cottage in Manchester?

ENGELS: Not Manchester no.

JENNY: Did you get anything?

NYM: Flour, coal, sausages.

ENGELS: Sausages, without money?

NYM: There's a butcher in Camden has a thing for desperate lady émigrés.

ENGELS: A thing?

NYM: His penis.

(NYM takes coal out of her pockets and drops it in the scuttle.)

JENNY: Which one followed you?

NYM: *(Pointing at the portraits.)* Him. One eye, two chins, no neck.

JENNY: There are more spies in Dean Street than whores. Doc Schmidt sketches them

ENGELS: But they can't touch us? The spies. The whores *can* touch us.

JENNY: We're alright. We're political refugees, we're free.

ENGELS: Only in England, so thank God for England. Set foot in Germany and your brother would lock us up and throw away the door.

JENNY: Don't call him my brother.

ENGELS: What do we call him?

NYM: The Prussian Minster of the Interior, or the arsehole.

NYM: Has Fawksey eaten?

JENNY: He wouldn't.

NYM: So is that a "no"?

JENNY: He wouldn't eat anything.

NYM: That last drop of soup?

JENNY: I tried. My child would not eat.

NYM: Let me try.

(Furious knocking at the door, Beethoven's fifth.)

JENNY: Moor.

(ENGELS unbolts the door. MARX bursts in.)

ENGELS: Mon brave!

MARX: General, this is not a good time for me to acknowledge how industrially overjoyed I am to see you, but I am.

(ENGELS throws open his arms, but MARX in haste climbs up chimney. Banging on the door.)

SGT SAVAGE: *(Off.)* Open up! Police!

(JENNY opens the door. The POLICEMAN comes in.)

JENNY: Hello.

SGT SAVAGE: Who lives here?

JENNY: Ich spreche kein Englisch, Constable.

SGT SAVAGE: *Constable* painted the Hay Wain.

ENGELS: Sergeant?

SGT SAVAGE: Two stripes.

JENNY: Entschuldigen Sie, bitte.

SGT SAVAGE: I'd love to but I don't drink on duty. What's your name ma'am?

ENGELS: Dein Name. *(Your name.)*

JENNY: Jenny von Westphalen.

SGT SAVAGE: And you sir?

ENGELS: I'm her husband. Friedrich…Engels. I kept my maiden name when we got married.

(NYM comes in and lights the fire, putting some bread dough in the oven.)

SGT SAVAGE: And you miss –

NYM: Was weiß ich?! *(What do I know.)*

(NYM leaves.)

SGT SAVAGE: Are you all German in here?

ENGELS: Ja, what can we do for you Sergeant?

SGT SAVAGE: I don't have eyes in the back of my head, so maybe you can help.

ENGELS: I can't help with that. I don't have eyes in the back of my head either.

(MARX coughs. SGT SAVAGE turns to ENGELS who quickly coughs into a hankie.)

JENNY: Was haben wir falsch gemacht? *(What did we do wrong.)*

ENGELS: Liebling, mach dir keine Sorgen. *(Honey, don't worry.)*

SGT SAVAGE: Looking for a thief. This one's dark, hairy, talks gibberish.

JENNY: Hat er einen Namen?

ENGELS: Do you have a name?

SGT SAVAGE: Sgt Savage.

ENGELS: For the thief?

SGT SAVAGE: Charles Marx or Monsieur Ramboz.

(The SERGEANT walks the room sniffing out hidden bodies. By the piano he is sure someone is hiding inside, so he hits a key.)

Middle C.

(NYM stokes the fire. The SERGEANT heads for one of the rooms. JENNY gets in his way.)

JENNY: Liebling, was tut er jetzt!? *(Darling, what's he doing now??)*

ENGELS: Mein wife wants to know if you're licensed to search private property without a warrant.

SGT SAVAGE: I dunno. Law enforcement, early days, it's all up for grabs.

(The SERGEANT inspects the rogue's gallery. ENGELS pulls NYM away from the fire. MARX coughs from up the chimney. ENGELS takes out a hankie and coughs into it.)

ENGELS: It's a hobby of my wife's. They're hanging up to dry.

SGT SAVAGE: They're pencil.

JENNY: Nasser Bleistift.

ENGELS: Wet pencil.

SGT SAVAGE: What's in here?

JENNY: Mein Sohn schlaft da drin! *(My son sleeps in there.)*

ENGELS: Our son is asleep in there.

SGT SAVAGE: We'll see if that's true.

(The SERGEANT opens the door and looks in without going in.)

Yes, he's still asleep.

(Closes the door loudly.)

FAWKSEY: *(Off.)* Mamma.

JENNY: Sie haben das Kind aufgeweckt! *(You've woken the child.)*

NYM: Soll ich zu ihm gehen? *(Do you want to go?)* *(To the SERGEANT.)* Idioten!

SERGEANT: What did she say?

ENGELS: She said maybe the idiot made it up to the roof?

SERGEANT: This villain may be highly dangerous, so if you see him, approach him, knock his lights out, then come and get one of us. Au revoir.

(The SERGEANT leaves. ENGELS closes the door. ENGELS laughs.)

NYM: Is Moor – ?

JENNY: Up the chimney.

NYM: I didn't know!

(She damps the fire down.)

ENGELS: Monsieur Ramboz! You can come down.

(MARX clambers out, laughing.)

MARX: *(Coughing/laughing.)* You utter bastardly bunch of bastards. That was such an unbelievably not very clever thing to do to a much loved friend, husband – und Hauptman!

(He falls into ENGELS' arms. It's an extended embrace of genuine affection. JENNY looks on and then continues packing. NYM continues making the fire/bread.)

ENGELS: You didn't reply to my letter from last week.

MARX: So depressed was I by the industrial scale of the negativity –

JENNY: – industrial and all its cognates is this month's favourite word.

MARX: Jennychen, we're not supposed to be talking.

JENNY: I was talking to him.

MARX: She's packing *again.* Where's my damned wine?!

ENGELS: Bordeaux in my pocket.

(ENGELS picks up a bottle from his overcoat and gives it to MARX who opens it straight away.)

MARX: Chateaux Margaux '46!?

ENGELS: D'accord! Courtesy of the philistine, my father. I write a good letter, I cry in ink.

MARX: Drink before you go darling? Wet the separation's head.

(MARX blocks JENNY on her way to the suitcase with more clothes.)

ENGELS: Moor, please –

MARX: – it's all for show.

(JENNY moves around MARX and deposits another pile of clothes into the suitcase.)

MARX: How was France?

ENGELS: It's one great big open air asylum. But still, without French women life wouldn't be worth living. Present company –

JENNY: – insulted!

(MARX blocks JENNY's path to the suitcases.)

MARX: Can we stop the cabaret? Woman has cried wolf before.

JENNY: I'm not crying wolf, I'm going.

(JENNY deposits more dresses in the suitcases.)

MARX: She's not adapted at all well to abject poverty.

JENNY: Ha!

MARX: Back in Trier, in the Von Westphalen mansion she had her own feathered four poster. I shared a small double with three siblings. Never slept on my own until I married her.

JENNY: In his inward looking universe, where every observation is fed by a prejudice in favour of the sole inhabitant, the needs and feelings of other human beings serve only to magnify and distort his bloated sense of personal torment.

MARX: She wanted to give that speech at our wedding. It was a traditional Prussian affair, military uniforms, guard of honour, firing squad.

ENGELS: What I can't understand is what you found attractive about him in the first place.

JENNY: I was given no choice. He bombarded me with poetry. Three volumes! He didn't buy them in a bookshop and wrap them nicely, he wrote them himself.

MARX: Only because it was cheaper.

ENGELS: I bet they were terrible.

JENNY: They were all perfectly beautiful. Though, shall we say, somewhat after Shelley. You know the style, where it can't be love unless there's more suffering than joy.

ENGELS: Not my kind of thing then.

JENNY: I know you've read Shelley.

ENGELS: Of course, but I didn't take it as a manifesto. I'm a materialist, earthbound, I can't handle all that spiritual mumbo jumbo.

MARX: Ask her why she's come back.

ENGELS: I blame you for marrying him. You were older, you're still older for that matter, and you should've known better.

JENNY: Like Shelley's Prometheus, I am bound to him.

MARX: Not tightly enough it seems.

JENNY: This is a private conversation! I am bound to him, and bound to revolution.

ENGELS: A double Prometheus.

JENNY: There are times when I believe the two to be separate entities, and times when they're one. And then there are the children. But you know love, and its complications.

ENGELS: I'm a shipwreck.

JENNY: You have a wonderful time.

ENGELS: Staggering from likes, to pleasures, to diversions?

JENNY: It's not enough?

ENGELS: I have no love that combines spirit, soul, intellect and desire.

(JENNY takes his hand.)

Moor, why do you think she's leaving?

MARX: I didn't pay the doctor's bill. For Fawksey. I don't have any respect for prosaic imperative exigencies such as paying bourgeois tricksters like the specialist Doctor William Whitehead who, incidentally, is suing me. The Hippocratic Oath – "don't give credit". Thus I am seeking paid employment with the creator of the perforated ticket stub, Isambard Kingdom Brunel.

ENGELS: Jenny tells me she's landed a contract with Meissner for the book.

MARX: So I'm a business now am I? A manufactory of words.

JENNY: And Polyakov in St. Petersburg.

MARX: Russia?!

ENGELS: What's wrong with Russia wanting the book?

MARX: A book about capitalism?! Russia's never had capitalism! There's more chance of a proletarian revolution starting in Windsor.

JENNY: Polyakov will pay an advance.

MARX: She wants me to turn revolution into money!?

ENGELS: Does the book have a title yet?

MARX: "Das Volkswirtschaft Scheisse".

ENGELS: The Economic Shit?

MARX: In English I'm inclined to drop the definite article.

ENGELS: "Economic Shit"?

MARX: Do you like it?

ENGELS: Five years, and all you've got is the title?! I've had some long craps in my time, but that takes the biscuit.

JENNY: You're wasting your time.

ENGELS: God –

MARX: – who!?

ENGELS: Although you killed him, God put you on earth to explain capitalism –

MARX: – I'll explain capitalism. The railway pays fifteen shillings a week, and the rent is only eight. What are the proletariat complaining about? We have a surplus of seven bob to spend on claret, and cigars.

JENNY: Food!

ENGELS: But Moor!?

MARX: I tried my hand at theatre criticism. There is no higher profession. At its best it combines intellect, spirit and compassion. But at its worst, you're just a bit of a twat.

ENGELS: The railway it is!

MARX: I shall be a great railway clerk, maybe the greatest ever. When I'm gone they'll build a huge statue of me outside Paddington station.

(FAWKSEY enters.)

MARX: Guido Fawksey Marx!

FAWKSEY: Daddy!

MARX: One day son, all this will be yours! Say hello, to Uncle Freddy.

FAWKSEY: *(From behind MARX's legs.)* Hello.

ENGELS: Hello little fellah!

FAWKSEY: *(Flexing his muscles.)* I'm big and strong now. Can you be a horse Daddy?

MARX: I am a horse!

(MARX gets down on all fours and puts FAWKSEY on his back.)

MARX: Hold on tight Sir Fawksey, only you can tame this bucking stallion.

FAWKSEY: Fence! Neighhhhhhhh, neighhhhhh!

(MARX rears up like a horse. FAWKSEY holds on, yelping with delight.)

River!

JENNY: Careful. You'll make him ill.

NYM: His throat is red raw.

(NYM takes FAWKSEY from MARX and sits him down by the fire.)

FAWKSEY: *(To ENGELS.)* Daddy's going to drive a train.

MARX: Yes and then we'll have all the food, and all the doctors, we need, won't we Fawksey!

JENNY: Doc Schmidt is coming to see him, later.

MARX: Sorry, are you still here?

(JENNY moves towards FAWKSEY, a maternal hand outstretched.)

JENNY: Fawksey darling. Mummy's going away, just for a while.

(MARX, the stallion rears up.)

MARX: Say goodbye to Mummy.

FAWKSEY: I don't want Mamma to go?!

(FAWKSEY starts crying. NYM steps in and comforts him. JENNY goes to look out of the window.)

MARX: Looking for someone?

JENNY: There's a Hackney cab coming for me.

MARX: Is your lover stumping up the cash?

ENGELS: Excuse me?

MARX: Willich?

ENGELS: August Willich?

JENNY: *(To ENGELS.)* August is not my lover. He's only doing what men do, pursuing the worm that lives in every marriage.

MARX: Johan August Ernst Von Willich and Johanna Berthe Julie Jenny Von Westphalen. They could have had the longest wedding invitations in Prussian history. Cigar?

(MARX offers ENGELS a cigar.)

ENGELS: Never known to refuse.

MARX: From a shyster Polak in Holborn, one and six a box, that's eight pence cheaper than my usuals, so every time I smoke a box, I'm saving eight pence. If I smoke three boxes a week I can live on my savings.

ENGELS: These cigars are execrable!

MARX: I'm glad you like them!

NYM: There's a League meeting tonight and –

ENGELS: – tonight?!

NYM: He won't go. Will you?

ENGELS: He will go, he will speak.

(JENNY sits and takes FAWKSEY off NYM.)

NYM: Do you know Emmanuel Barthélemy? He's come over from France.

ENGELS: Loony Manny. Course I know him.

MARX: He's as mad as a spoon. As a child he was bitten by a dog.

ENGELS: He was alright but the dog died of rabies.

MARX: Marx and Engels!

ENGELS: Engels and Marx!

MARX: My wife's packing, she's travelling to Italy.

ENGELS: Genoa?

MARX: Of course I know her, she's my wife. She's going with Willich.

ENGELS: August?

MARX: Through to December. Marx and Engels!

ENGELS: Engels and Marx!

(MARX and ENGELS dance around the room in a music hall routine, finding and donning hats and using pokers from the fire as canes.)

MARX/ENGELS: *(Scat.)* Da, da, da, dadadada, de da de da da, de da da, ta daaaa!

FAWKSEY: Daddy's silly!

(ENGELS looks to JENNY. She looks back, defiant then rises from her chair and deliberately goes and retrieves her cases. She really is going.)

NYM: Barthélemy and Willich! That's the double act we should be worried about!

MARX: August Willich!? He couldn't start a revolution, he can't even fuck my wife, and he's been trying for ten years.

JENNY: Fifteen.

MARX: I gave him five off for appalling behaviour.

NYM: Is anyone listening to me?! Our people here, the refugees, are tolerated, I'm not saying we're accepted. But Barthélemy, he's different, he's unstable, he's unpredictable –

ENGELS: – he's French.

NYM: And he's not on his own, he's brought the League of the Just with him.

ENGELS: Is this true?

NYM: Yes, those bloodthirsty fanatics. He will start an inferno. And then leave. And the English will blame us, and we will suffer the consequences.

FAWKSEY: Can you be a train Daddy?

MARX: Yes, Fawksey. Though my train's the same as my horse.

(MARX takes FAWKSEY for a train ride around the room, clambering over chairs and tables, making train noises. FAWKSEY yelps in delight.)

ENGELS: Moor, you know you must speak at the meeting! The League of the Just are here because they can smell weakness.

NYM: They must know you've stepped aside.

MARX: Excuse me General. All aboard!

FAWKSEY: Bridge!

MARX: Tunnel!!

NYM: Moor! He's not well! Stop it!

MARX: We don't stop till Doncaster!

(NYM plonks herself directly in MARX's way, blocking him.)

NYM: Give him to me!

MARX: Prussian housemaid on the line!

(MARX hands FAWKSEY back to NYM who takes him back into the bedroom and then returns.)

ENGELS: Write something, for tonight. I'll read it.

MARX: I can't write! I can't sit down.

JENNY: Boils.

MARX: I have boils on my arse so big that they have arses of their own, with boils on.

(MARX pulls his pants down and shows ENGELS his arse.)

ENGELS: Urgh, I've seen some disgusting backsides –

MARX: – clean though.

ENGELS: You could eat your lunch off it.

MARX: I like to keep a clean arse in case one of these Prussian beauties has a moment of weakness.

JENNY: He lances the boils himself with a razor.

MARX: Because my loving wife refused. *I promise to take you Karl Heinrich Marx to be my husband from this day forward to join with you and share in all that is to come!* Your words!

(MARX demonstrates.)

Hand held mirror; razor arm through the legs, slit the bastard, clean the mirror; go again.

NYM: He has to stand at the British Museum, people think he's an exhibit.

MARX: General, go and flag her a Hackney will you.

ENGELS: No!

MARX: You want out of a marriage, call a cab.

JENNY: Nym, remember to give Fawksey the cough syrup Doc Schmidt prescribed?

21

NYM: First thing in the morning and before he sleeps.

MARX: Do leave a forwarding address. We won't trouble you with anything below diphtheria. Certainly not pneumonia, there's quite a high survival rate nowadays.

ENGELS: Enough! Nym's right, if Willich and Barthélemy start a botched revolution here in England, our only refuge, our freedom, no, our lives are at stake. So put those sausages away. Now, for six months past I have not had a single opportunity to make use of my acknowledged gift for mixing a lobster salad – quelle horreur; it makes one quite rusty.

JENNY: Nym won't eat fish.

ENGELS: Another acknowledged gift of mine is roast leg of lamb. Nym?

NYM: Smashing.

ENGELS: Lamb. And we're going to eat together, and we're going to talk. Is that agreed?

(There is a knock at the door.)

MARX: Doc Schmidt. Our German doctor and comrade!

(MARX lets in SCHMIDT.)

SCHMIDT: Frau Marx. Moor. Comrade Nym! Herr Engels! Good to see friendly faces. Good to see faces. I've administered three enemas today. I think I washed my hands.

JENNY: He's in the bedroom.

SCHMIDT: Why is every revolutionary émigré in London constipated? My theory is that they're all suffering under the sheer intellectual strain of understanding your prose Herr Marx. Either that or we're eating too many eggs.

SCHMIDT: How's your cock?

ENGELS: It's fine. Thanks for asking.

SCHMIDT: Cleared up?

ENGELS: Yes. It's like new again.

SCHMIDT: Ha! Your secret's safe with me. Coming to the meeting?

ENGELS: Certainly.

SCHMIDT: That arrogant bastard won't come.

ENGELS: I'm working on it.

SCHMIDT: *(Producing sketches.)* Three new spies. Uglier than the last lot. I had to sketch them at intervals just so I could keep my lunch down.

(SCHMIDT places the new sketches on the dado rail alongside the existing 'rogues'.)

(To JENNY.) I have a new theory, the Prussian Minister of the Interior –

JENNY: – my brother. Don't be polite Gertie.

SCHMIDT: He wants his revenge on Moor for marrying you.

MARX: He calls it the "Trier Incident".

SCHMIDT: I sympathise. His sister decides to marry not just a penniless Jew, but a penniless Jew intent on destroying the Prussian monarchy.

FAWKSEY: *(Off.)* Mamma!

(FAWKSEY is crying.)

SCHMIDT: The patient calls! Think of the fees! Oh, but you don't pay.

(SCHMIDT opens his valise and takes out his stethoscope, and puts it round his neck.)

Any change in symptoms?

JENNY: The cough's harder.

(SCHMIDT, and JENNY go into the bedroom.)

NYM: Moor! I need to speak to you. Alone.

MARX: He's not important.

ENGELS: I love you too.

(There is a knock at the main door. MARX and NYM look at each other with concern.)

MARX: No?

NYM: No.

(MARX goes in the cupboard.)

NYM: Who is it?

SCHRAMM: *(Off.)* It's me!

NYM: Herr Schramm?!

MARX: *(From the cupboard.)* Tell him I'm dead.

(NYM opens the door and CONRAD SCHRAMM enters.)

SCHRAMM: A most felicitous day to you Comrade Nym.

NYM: Hello Conrad.

SCHRAMM: And Herr Engels, an additional pleasure of the most joyous kind.

ENGELS: Good to see you.

(SCHRAMM goes to the cupboard. ENGELS laughs helplessly.)

Guten Tag Herr Doktor Marx!

MARX: *(From within the cupboard.)* I'm not in here!

SCHRAMM: I apologise. Forgive my presumption, born as it is, of enthusiasm and warm fellowship.

(JENNY enters from the upstage left room.)

JENNY: He's stopped coughing. Doc Schmidt just picked him up.

MARX: *(From within.)* The man's a genius!

SCHRAMM: Madame Marx, radiance has found a new face, and calls itself Madame Marx.

JENNY: Conrad, how nice to see you. Doc Schmidt needs honey for the syrup.

NYM: I'll get it.

(JENNY goes back into the bedroom.)

ENGELS: What news of the Zeitung?

SCHRAMM: Since Herr Marx did me the unfathomable honour of appointing me as his successor editor of the New Rheinische Zeitung I have been working ceaselessly on the re-launch.

ENGELS: And you have proofs, an edition to show us?

MARX: Which you can leave on the table.

SCHRAMM: Indubitably. I have not yet an edition sir, but I have made progress on the relaunch title.

MARX: *(From within.)* I'm all ears.

SCHRAMM: Indeed sir, and I dare to hope that you will heartily approve. The organ, which I am honoured to edit, was named by you, in a stroke of unparalleled genius, as successor to the original Rheinischer Zeitung, the New Rheinischer Zietung! I have been touched, I hope, by my own muse, in humbly suggesting, for it is but a suggestion, that the London edition should be relaunched –

MARX: – Schramm!? You are trespassing upon eternity!

ENGELS: What is your suggested title?

SCHRAMM: The New New Rheinischer Zeitung!

(Silence. MARX emerges from the cupboard.)

MARX: New, New? Who knew?

ENGELS: It's brilliant!

(MARX moves to SCHRAMM and begins propelling him towards the door.)

SCHRAMM: Herr Doktor Marx, it is, as a title, a developing work in progress, there is more! I –

MARX: – Shoo! Out!

SCHRAMM: I apologise, I have six other suggested possible titles.

MARX: No! Get out!

(They slightly manhandle SCHRAMM out of the door.)

MARX: If I had a choice to get rid of Schramm or my boils, I'd keep the boils. He worships me! I can't bear it!

ENGELS: You love it, worship, and you appointed him.

MARX: Never make editorial appointments when completely pissed.

(Enter SCHMIDT from the upstage left room. JENNY follows. NYM comes from the kitchen with the honey.)

How's Fawksey?

SCHMIDT: Croup. Continue with the borax.

JENNY: And the honey?

SCHMIDT: Coat the back of his throat, if he won't tolerate that, put some on his tongue.

NYM: I'll try it now.

JENNY: No, let him sleep a little. Then I'll do it.

MARX: Ah, she's staying.

JENNY: I need to eat. And then I'm leaving.

ENGELS: Leg of lamb, potatoes, parsnips, butter. Any requests?

MARX: Bit of foie gras?

ENGELS: Or pâté de campagne.

BOTH: Both!

(ENGELS leaves.)

SCHMIDT: You know the League of the Just have sent a contingent over from Paris.

MARX: Let the lunatics run the asylum!

SCHMIDT: And allow these hot heads to take over?!

NYM: Who's on the door tonight?

SCHMIDT: I'll do that, armed if necessary, but I don't know the European membership.

MARX: They're all members.

NYM: We have a list.

(NYM leaves to the upstage right bedroom, and comes back with the lists.)

SCHMIDT: Will you be there Frau Marx?

JENNY: When have I ever missed a meeting?

SCHMIDT: Mein Fuhrer?

MARX: What does this have to do with trains!?

SCHMIDT: They shot the King of Prussia two days ago.

JENNY: Is he dead?

SCHMIDT: A bullet wound. He survived. And now they're here, with designs on Queen Victoria.

NYM: That would be the end for us Moor.

SCHMIDT: Would you allow this beautiful movement that you founded, for which you are the inspiration, and for which I cure the constipation… that has given us a just purpose to our lives…this evening of all evenings… what is it that is keeping you away?

MARX: I'm going to drink a pint in every pub on Tottenham Court Road.

SCHMIDT: Oh dear, you're an arsehole, and I know about arseholes.

NYM: Herr Engels will speak, as will I.

MARX: Jenny, will you speak?

JENNY: No.

(NYM gives SCHMIDT the lists.)

NYM: Each name has a number. If someone gives a name, ask them for their number.

SCHMIDT: Thank you. Moor, I beg of you, for those comrades who died in '48, please come. Auf Wiedersehen.

(SCHMIDT leaves. The door is bolted again by NYM.)

NYM: You should be ashamed.

MARX: I have a far bigger task ahead of me. There are eighteen pubs on Tottenham Court Road.

NYM: Karl, we must talk!

MARX: All we ever do in this house is talk. What is it? *(Pause.)* What?

(A knock on the door, coded.)

Qui Qui! Everyone be upstanding for the Emperor of China!

(MARX lets in QUI QUI.)

QUI QUI: I saw Uncle Freddy in the street!

JENNY: Qui Qui! How was school?

(She ignores JENNY and goes to the piano.)

QUI QUI: Is he staying?!

MARX: He'll stay for dinner. He's paying for it.

(QUI QUI goes straight to the piano.)

QUI QUI: I've learned a new piece by John Field.

MARX: Bloody English music!

QUI QUI: John Field is Irish daddy.

MARX: The Irish *are* English, Act of Union 1801.

(They laugh. QUI QUI plays Op 51 Sehnsuchts-Walzer. There is banging at the door.)

JENNY: No!

NYM: Keep playing!

MARX: I'm beginning to sympathise with cuckoos, the Swiss ones, that live in clocks.

(MARX hides in the cupboard. QUI QUI continues.)

JENNY: Who is it?

GRABINER: Mister Grabiner!

(JENNY lets in the BAILIFF and two PORTERS. NYM is in the kitchen.)

JENNY: The bailiffs! Mister Grabiner.

BAILIFF: I was only saying to my trouble and strife this morning that I spend more time with that Mrs Marx than I do with her.

JENNY: Take a seat.

BAILIFF: Thank you.

(He picks up a chair, hands it to a PORTER, and the PORTER walks out the flat with it.)

JENNY: That is our one good chair. Who is it today?

BAILIFF: Mrs Gertrude Price, the landlady. The rent never sleeps. What does your husband do all day? If you can't find work in London, you must be neither use nor ornament.

NYM: Mister Marx spends all day in this cupboard.

(She opens the door. MARX is revealed.)

MARX: Guten morgen.

BAILIFF: Morning.

MARX: Close the door Nym, I'm beginning to quake.

(NYM closes the door.)

JENNY: The landlady, anyone else?

BAILIFF: Mrs Eileen Wilson, piano lessons, unpaid.

(MARX opens the cupboard door and steps out.)

MARX: She teaches mein daughter Irish scrapings und then has the nerve to sue!

BAILIFF: It won't happen again, 'cause the piano's going. Lads!

(The two PORTERS approach the piano. QUI QUI cries and steps aside. MARX hits the keys with Beethoven's 5th.)

BAILIFF: Piano, fifteen shillings.

JENNY: It's a Broadwood.

QUI QUI: Daddy!

BAILIFF: Fifteen shillings and sixpence. Take it away lads.

MARX: You English can take the bread from out of our mouths, aber nie, you can't take our culture!

BAILIFF'S ASSISTANT: Where do I know you from?

MARX: The British Museum?

BAILIFF'S ASSISTANT: I know, you play the Joanna in the King's Head.

PORTER 2: He's quite good.

(The lads wheel the piano out of the flat with MARX still playing it, when they get to the door, he has to jump on the top of it in order to continue playing, which he does, B's 5th still. The piano, PORTERS and MARX all leave but are heard off arguing / playing. The PORTERS come back in without MARX, who is now playing some Schubert out in the street.)

BAILIFF: One kettle. One shilling.

JENNY: No! You know the law Mr Grabiner. Necessities of life!

(GRABINER puts the kettle back down.)

BAILIFF: Mozart?

PORTER: Beethoven! Opus 67!

PORTER 2: Quality dresses these guv.

JENNY: Herr Grabiner, diese Kleider are mine, I was …

BAILIFF: – doing a runner?

JENNY: Nein!

(The PORTERS come out of the bedroom with a child's cot and place it before the BAILIFF.)

FAWKSEY: Mamma! My bed!

BAILIFF: One child's bed.

JENNY: Bitte! Leave the bed, he's not well. Take die Klieder.

BAILIFF: A shilling each. The bed two shillings.

JENNY: Do you not have a heart?

BAILIFF: I'm a bailiff.

JENNY: I have a silver piece, an Argyll, very, very valuable.

(JENNY takes a screwdriver and starts desperately raising the floorboard.)

Solid silver, and in here.

(JENNY lifts the floorboard. She lifts out a cloth, but no silver.)

Nym! It's gone.

NYM: My God no.

BAILIFF: Take the bed lads.

JENNY: Where is it?

(The PORTERS take the cot, children's clothes and the linen out passing MARX in the doorway. JENNY is on her knees and then lets out a scream.)

Moor?

BAILIFF: Take the bed lads.

JENNY: Moor!?

End of Scene.

SCENE FOUR

(In a Soho Street. People go about their business, some émigrés in huddles. A SPY is lurking on a street corner.

MRS MULLET: Winkles, whelks and oysters!

MARX: Do you own diese whelk stall?

MRS MULLET: Na. I rent the cart, shilling and six a week off my father in law; I got a lease on the pitch here, that's two shilling a month to the council –

MARX: – but diese whelks are yours? Your husband's ein fisherman?

MRS MULLET: Fuck off! Cowans of Barking, they give me thirty pints of whelks of a morning, and I get sixpence for every pint I sell, and a tuppeny penalty for every pint I don't sell. For the oysters –

MARX: – nein, nein, stop! It's already too complicated.

(Enter ENGELS followed by a SPY. ENGELS grabs MARX.)

ENGELS: Moor! Come here!

MARX: No, I have an important and unfinished pub crawl to continue. See you there.

ENGELS: Who's that?

MARX: Let me introduce my personal spy.

(Shouted.) Evening Helmut!

HELMUT: Good evening Herr Marx.

MARX: This is my tailor, Godfrey Schnitzelgrueberleinchenlein.

HELMUT: Looks like Friedrich Engels to me.

MARX: So that explains the short sleeves!

HELMUT: Red Lion league meeting tonight?

MARX: I've seen the light, given up revolution. Start work Monday, with Great Western.

HELMUT: The railway?

MARX: I tried to change the world, I failed, but I will transform Paddington station. Tell your boss, my brother-in-law, that he needn't worry about me in future. He can focus fully on his halitosis.

(HELMUT moves off. MARX starts walking.)

ENGELS: The Red Lion's that way.

MARX: But the King's Head is this way.

ENGELS: You've no money for drink, unless you got cash for the Argyll?

MARX: Not a penny from the pawnbroker.

ENGELS: You still have the Argyll then?

MARX: I don't have money and I don't have the Argyll!

ENGELS: Do you know anything about pawnbroking? She's furious!

(MARX starts walking off.)

ENGELS: If Victoria is assassinated they'll arrest Jenny, Nym, Qui Qui and Fawksey!

(ENGELS walks off upstage towards the Red Lion.)

MRS MULLET: Thames oysters! Surprise the wife!

ENGELS: Are they good oysters?

MRS MULLET: Put it this way, my husband had five last night and three of them worked.

(Enter NYM and JENNY.)

NYM: There are no genuinely working-class artisans. Not one shipyard worker, no foundry men, not a single miner.

JENNY: Nym, we're in Soho.

NYM: A rag tag mob of refugee revolutionaries.

JENNY: Qui Qui knows how to do the borax and honey?

NYM: I showed her, someone had to show her.

(JENNY stops in her tracks.)

JENNY: Nym, will you just stop it.

NYM: Stop what?

JENNY: Judging me!

NYM: Why do –

JENNY: – I cannot be everything. His wife, his scrivener, his publishing agent, the perfect mother.

NYM: I have never judged you as a mother. I admire you. How could I not? You're a founder, an original signatory. That's why you must speak tonight. They listen to you.

JENNY: Nym, what's happened.

NYM: What do you mean? Nothing's happened.

JENNY: You've been behaving, recently, not like Nym. You're not you.

NYM: I am me. I just carry on. I'm fine.

JENNY: I'm not going to argue. I've known you for ten years. You're not *fine*.

WILLICH: *(Off.)* Jenny.

NYM: I'm going to speak tonight, but they'll want to hear from you. Speak.

(WILLICH appears. He and JENNY nod recognition. NYM sees him, knows him.)

I'll see you in there.

(NYM looks at WILLICH and then moves off towards the Red Lion.)

WILLICH: Why didn't you come?

JENNY: The bailiffs took everything.

WILLICH: I would take you with nothing. Where is he?

JENNY: I don't know.

WILLICH: He uses you.

JENNY: For what?

WILLICH: Money, from your family.

JENNY: They've stopped giving.

WILLICH: Your handwriting.

JENNY: Ha! Every revolutionary cell needs someone with beautiful handwriting.

WILLICH: Is he coming? Tonight?

JENNY: He said not.

WILLICH: Then we can make progress. Are you with us?

JENNY: I don't know what you plan. But I will listen.

WILLICH: You could stay with me tonight.

JENNY: August –

(WILLICH gestures to her to stop.)

WILLICH: I exist on hope. That's how love works.

(They head on to the Red Lion.)

End of Scene.

SCENE FIVE

(The upstairs function room of the Red Lion. Alive with émigrés of both sexes. Talk, shouting, drinking, laughter. SCHMIDT is on the door. SCHRAMM, ENGELS, NYM and others. A German workers' song.)

SONG the Marseillaise in German

SCHMIDT: Comrades!

WILLICH: Where is Marx?

TERRORISTS: Yes!? / Where is he!? / Is he with us!?

ENGELS: Comrade Marx told me he would be late.

TERRORISTS: Bourgeois coward / apologist! / He's in the museum!

BARTHÉLEMY: Is there something more urgent than the overthrow of the monarchy!?

WILLICH: Comrades! The Fox! Escaped from the galleys only last week. Emmanuel Barthélemy!

(Some cheers. BARTHÉLEMY kisses WILLICH.)

And he kisses like a horse!

BARTHÉLEMY: Messieurs Dames! Bon soir! I am, how you say, prêt?

WILLICH: Ready.

BARTHÉLEMY: I am ready, prêt, ready. England is prêt, ready, for revolution. And our weapon, it is a technique, technique?

WILLICH: Technique.

BARTHÉLEMY: Le technique is le terrorisme, c'est quoi?

WILLICH: Terror.

BARTHÉLEMY: The Terror!?

WILLICH: Just terror, no definite article.

BARTHÉLEMY: Terror! We kill au hasard?

WILLICH: – at random.

BARTHÉLEMY: Soldiers, police, their wives, dans la rue! –

WILLICH: – in the street.

BARTHÉLEMY: – dans la gare!

WILLICH: In the stations.

BARTHÉLEMY: – dans les étangs!

WILLICH: – in the lakes?!

BARTHÉLEMY: In the lakes, en avant, encore, au hasard?

WILLICH: At random.

BARTHÉLEMY: Kill at random, the terror, we kill ici, là bas, en face!

WILLICH: Here, there and opposite.

BARTHÉLEMY: Encore, au hasard!?

WILLICH: At random!

BARTHÉLEMY: At random!

TERRORISTS: *(Cheer.)*

SCHMIDT: Helene De Muth. Nym.

NYM: There is a time for violence.

BARTHÉLEMY: A girl speaking!?

JENNY: A founder member of the League!

NYM: Kill Victoria and the English will turn against us. I am not against violence, and I will be there when that time comes, fighting beside you. But we are few, and the English workers love their Queen, they will not join us, they will hate us.

TERRORIST: – to the streets!

JENNY: – we are not ready! When we are ready! When!

BARTHÉLEMY: I am prêt! Now!

WILLICH: The English proletariat are ready but they need leadership, an act to fire this nation out of its complacency! A spark!

BARTHÉLEMY: Kill, au hasard!

MARX: *(Entering.)* You killed a policeman in Paris, au hasard. What good did that do?

BARTHÉLEMY: Monsieur Marx!?

MARX: Voilà! It got you ten years on the galleys. Comrades, do you know what ten years on the galleys is?! It's a fuck of a lot of rowing!

WILLICH: You're drunk!

MARX: But not insane. So August Willich, this is your big idea, to use this French attack dog as a spark?

BARTHÉLEMY: A match to fire Europe!

MARX: And we will all die in the fire.

(Mumbles of discontent.)

Have you seen the British army? They're a machine, a mindless, grinding machine that will crush us. Comrade Marx, have you spoken?

JENNY: Comrades, we have an opportunity here. Fate has brought us to England. To this most advanced industrialised society with a vast city-living proletariat, oppressed, exploited, ripe to be educated which will bring them to us. Violence will turn them away.

MARX: '48 was a lesson and only idiots do not learn. And are we idiots?! Most of us are not. Time, which was invented just down the road here in Greenwich, only three years ago, is on our side. We use this time to prepare, to be ready –

BARTHÉLEMY: Ready?

WILLICH: – prêt.

MARX: – ready for power, because there will be a moment, in the future, a moment when the markets have crashed, the banks do not open their doors on this day, because they are bust. The money has eaten itself. And on this day there will be a beautiful void, and truth coalesces around a void, and that void will be filled by the universal truth that every man and every woman has the right not to be exploited by any other man or woman. And on this day the soldiers will not have been paid, the police will not have been paid, and without wages they will not defend capitalism, so we will not have to break down the doors, they'll give us the keys, and we'll walk in. And all class antagonisms will be swept aside, and the proletariat will become the ruling class, no! Not the ruling class, there will be no classes, and all men and women will be equal and we will have a socialist association in which the free development of each is the free development of all, and we will have a more honest and just way for our species to live.

WILLICH: Change cannot happen without violence!

TERRORIST: When will the economic crash come?

MARX: Tomorrow, but not today!

ÉMIGRÉ 2: We are sick of waiting!?

MARX: We are not waiting, we are making preparations for that day!

BARTHÉLEMY: But we are soldiers.

WILLICH: Your friend, the cotton lord, Herr Engels was there on the Elberfeld barricade in '48. Where were you Marx?

MARX: Engels tells me he fought in four skirmishes under your command all of which were futile and involved a great loss of life.

WILLICH: Where were you?!

BARTHÉLEMY: In the pissing room of the British Museum!

MARX: There are voices within our movement that want nothing more than to see Europe burn; these sirens offer you death, an abattoir, where you are the meat.

BARTHÉLEMY: Jewish coward!

(Uproar. MARX lunges at BARTHÉLEMY. The two are pulled apart.)

ENGELS: Coward, no! Jewish, yes, like Christ!

BARTHÉLEMY: You think he's Christ!? I have news for you, I am Christ!

(BARTHÉLEMY produces two pistols.)

WILLICH: Marx is a coward!

MARX: Debatable, but I'm not an idiot.

BARTHÉLEMY: Are you calling Willich an idiot?

MARX: I said "I'm not an idiot".

WILLICH: Unlike me?!

MARX: Alright! If you insist! I'm not an idiot, unlike you!

TERRORIST: Who's he calling an idiot!?

WILLICH: Are you calling me an idiot!

(WILLICH lunges at MARX.)

MARX: You are an uneducated, priapic Prussian prick of an idiot.

BARTHÉLEMY: Priapic?

SCHMIDT: Always er… prêt.

(BARTHÉLEMY resists disarmament but puts his pistols away.)

WILLICH: Do you accuse me of something, with this woman?!

MARX: I do.

WILLICH: What of my honour?!

MARX: What of my honour!? And she's not *this woman*, she's my wife!

(The room hushes.)

JENNY: I can speak for my own honour!

MARX: If your honour exists it has no blood, no substance, unlike the lives of the men and women in this room which you, with unbound profligacy, will piss away on your own vain, narcissistic fantasy of a peacock's death!

WILLICH: As a gentleman, I demand satisfaction! I shall await you at dawn, on Hampstead Heath –

ALL: No / stop this now / we are comrades etc

WILLICH: A gentleman has a right to protect his honour.

BARTHÉLEMY: Choose your weapon Marx!

MARX: The pen! Pens at dawn!

BARTHÉLEMY: What!?

MARX: Debate, ideas, argument!

WILLICH: I'm going to kill you! Be there, dog, or I will come for you!

MARX: I'll be there, likewise dog.

JENNY: Moor. Just go home.

SCHRAMM: Herr Doktor Marx, please! Let us return to the business of the League.

ENGELS: Comrades this is not intelligent.

(WILLICH and BARTHÉLEMY leave. JENNY turns to go with them.)

WILLICH: Jenny!

MARX: Ha!

JENNY: You stole from me.

MARX: What?! The Argyll, no, I can get that back.

NYM: Jenny?! Please.

JENNY: *(To NYM.)* Don't let him go to the duel. He will be killed.

MARX: No!

(JENNY makes to leave. MARX stands to follow her. ENGELS and SCHMIDT hold him back.)

SCHRAMM: Comrades! Remember, tickets for the German Workers' Educational Society ball on Saturday at the Huguenot Hall are selling fast! See me or Doc Schmidt!

SCHMIDT: Meeting adjourned.

End of Scene.

SCENE SIX

(Soho Square with St. Patrick's Roman Catholic Church upstage with an opening where a door/gate should be, a hedge and then a pavement. Enter MARX, ENGELS, and DOC SCHMIDT, all drunk. MARX and ENGELS are carrying a large outdoor door or gate.)

MARX: The golden thread that bound Neanderthal man, through the earliest agrarian societies –

(ENGELS stops.)

ENGELS: – Moor! Stop talking! Write it down. Preferably in a book.

MARX: You wanted it explained you bugger!

ENGELS: I wanted to know why we've stolen a gate.

SCHMIDT: It's metonymic, a symbol.

ENGELS: It's a bloody heavy symbol.

MARX: Society was stable, exchange and barter were the norm. Then the Phoenicians, sick of slipping a goat in your back pocket in order to buy a pint, introduced a commodity of universal exchange.

ENGELS: Garden gates?

SCHMIDT: Cash.

MARX: Money!

ENGELS: Yes, but WHY HAVE WE STOLEN THIS BASTARD GATE?!

MARX: Because there comes a time in every man's life, when you've just got to nick a gate for a laugh.

(They all laugh. And drop the gate.)

SCHMIDT: What would that pawnbroker on Berwick Street give you for a gate like this?

MARX: Fuck all.

SCHMIDT: Which is twice as much as he gave you for that silver Argyll.

ENGELS: How d'you know he got half of fuck all for the Argyll?

SCHMIDT: I guessed. I'm going. I don't mind being arrested for sedition but drunk in charge of a gate, no.

MARX: *(Hugs him.)* Doc! You're the best of men.

SCHMIDT: Comrade.

MARX: I love you much more than that rich arsehole.

(SCHMIDT leaves.)

ENGELS: Who's a rich arsehole?

MARX: You! You fucking cotton lord. Ermen and Engels.

ENGELS: Oh I see, and which one of Ermen and Engels do you think is me?

MARX: Er… tough one. Engels?

ENGELS: No.

MARX: Ermen? You're Ermen?!

ENGELS: In Ermen and Engels I am neither Ermen nor Engels.

MARX: I don't understand.

ENGELS: I am not my father. When I worked there I was a wages clerk. The wages clerk does not get his name on the chimney.

MARX: Argh…don't give me that.

ENGELS: I drink good wine, yes, I hunt, I have my own hunter, yes, but only because I write begging letters to a father I detest, a philistine, and I pack every letter with lies and false affection.

MARX: I write him begging letters too.

ENGELS: My father?

MARX: Yes. Twice a week. I explain that I'm your best friend, and I tell him I love him.

ENGELS: Does he send you money?

MARX: No. Fucker.

ENGELS: You're taking the piss.

MARX: Piss! I knew there was something I had to do.

(MARX stands and goes for a piss.)

ENGELS: I hate Manchester. I'm never going back.

(ENGELS joins MARX for a piss.)

MARX: Marx and Engels!

ENGELS: Engels and Marx!

(They piss.)

MARX: You're pissing higher than me!

ENGELS: Because you're an intellectual, and I'm a machine for converting beer into piss.

MARX: Let me see your cock!

(MARX turns his head to looks at ENGELS, ready to argue.)

ENGELS: Don't turn towards me! We can do this conversation in profile.

MARX: Freddy, I've known you since Paris 1844 and I've never seen it.

ENGELS: It's a perfectly normal Prussian penis –

MARX: – you're using two hands!? You've got a cock like a fucking horse!

ENGELS: It's long and thin, like pipe cleaner.

(A POLICE OFFICEr appears strolling his beat.)

ENGELS: Peeler!

(ENGELS and MARX hastily stop pissing.)

CON CRIMP: Evening lads.

ENGELS: Guten abend evening Constable.

CON CRIMP: What we got here?

MARX: Ein gate.

ENGELS: Officer, I can explain –

MARX: – mein gate.

(The officer examines the back of the gate, which MARX and ENGELS can't now see.)

CON CRIMP: And where do you live?

MARX: I live behind diese gate.

CON CRIMP: And when you go for a drink, you take your gate with you?

MARX: Doesn't everyone?

ENGELS: I apologise for my friend.

(MARX starts to move round to look at the address. The OFFICER stops him.)

CON CRIMP: So this address here on the front is your address?

MARX: Jawohl!

CON CRIMP: What is it then?

MARX: Number one.

CON CRIMP: No.

(OFFICER shakes head after each number. ENGELS sits it out giggling.)

MARX: Two? Three? Fifty-six?

ENGELS: Constable, we'll take the gate back.

MARX: Seventy-two.

CON CRIMP: St. Patrick's Roman Catholic Church, Soho Square.

CON CRIMP: That's this church, and that'll be the hole.

ENGELS: I bloody told you we were going round in circles!

CON CRIMP: Lads. I'll be back in half an hour.

ENGELS: Thank you. For using your discretion. And for not hitting us.

CON CRIMP: I've been on a course.

(OFFICER walks off. During the next dialogue MARX and ENGELS put the door back on, possibly upside down.)

ENGELS: I will not let this duel happen.

MARX: No, I'm gonna kill him! My wife walked out of the Red Lion with him, in front of all of Europe.

ENGELS: Willich may love Jenny, but Jenny does not love Willich. Men fall in love with her looks, it's the tedious inconvenience of her life. I don't know why she went off with him. Who does?

MARX: Women.

ENGELS: Yeah.

MARX: I've starved our marriage, killed it, every day with a thousand penurious indignities. She's a bloody princess! I can't expect her to live like this! She would've been better off with you.

ENGELS: Yes.

MARX: What?

ENGELS: Yes.

MARX: What was my question?

ENGELS: You said Jenny would've been better off with me, and I said "yes". I would've given her what she wants.

MARX: A pony.

ENGELS: But that wouldn't be enough.

MARX: Two ponies?

ENGELS: Willich is a cavalry officer, he's got loads of ponies.

MARX: And he smells of horses. I can't compete with that.

ENGELS: Jenny wants you.

MARX: But I'm a disaster area. I am the opposite of King
Midas, everything I touch turns to debts. I have applied
my mind to the analysis of political economy and I can
see that history is determined by the economic relations
between classes, and if I can communicate this to the world
I know it will bring understanding and change, but I can't
pay the fucking butcher. I am defeated, brutalised –

ENGELS: – brutalised!?

MARX: Brutalised. I can't –

ENGELS: – you're not fucking brutalised you bourgeois prick.

MARX: Did you just call me a bourgeois prick?

ENGELS: Brutalised? Really, you can't use that word.

MARX: You're the word keeper now are you?

ENGELS: Go to Manchester. Then you'll see *brutalised.*

MARX: I'm sorry. I read your book. I couldn't put it down.

ENGELS: Fuck the book.

MARX: I apologise for reading your book.

ENGELS: I want you to smell it! And then to retch it up.

MARX: I know –

ENGELS: – you don't know anything! A mile from where
Mary lives there's a courtyard – I have never seen such
a concentration of degradation, sickness and filth. Fifty
families, one toilet between ten houses, the yard flows
with piss and shit, human shit, and the kids play in this
filth, barefoot. The parents of these kids are not there, no,
they're in the mill, all day every day, utterly consumed
by a task which is regimented and repetitive, the noise
is constant, they can't hear another human voice. An

existence more unnatural cannot be imagined. They are brutalised, and unlike you, they have no choices, and no prospect of escape except death. And if you'd ever stepped inside a mill or a manufactory you wouldn't dare use the word brutalised to describe your own life.

MARX: You're right. I'm a dick.

ENGELS: Solipsistic, self regarding prick. And if you don't write the Economic Shit, if you get a job, if you get shot in a duel, what about those people?! They need you. I can only observe, I write down what I see. I'm a beta plus. You're an alpha, a bona fide genius, you prick. You do that other thing, the analysis, the unlocking, the reveal.

(ENGELS stands and makes to leave.)

MARX: Alright, I'll make a research trip to Manchester.

ENGELS: Brutalised? Tch! What an arsehole.

(ENGELS walks off.)

And put that gate back!

End of Scene.

SCENE SEVEN

(Later that same night. The flat in a low light, seemingly deserted. Various possessions are strewn around the floor as there are no cabinets or tables or chairs. A sleepy FAWKSEY enters from the bedroom trailing a blanket, stops in the centre of the room, looks around.)

FAWKSEY: Mama?

(NYM in a night shift comes from the bedroom.)

NYM: Little one.

FAWKSEY: Where's Mama?

(NYM gathers FAWKSEY up.)

NYM: Come in my arms. You need to sleep. Then your mama will be here.

(NYM carries FAWKSEY back to bed. A few seconds pass. The sound of the door knob being turned and turned again in frustration when it is clear that the door is locked. Knocking on the door. Banging on the door.)

MARX: *(Off.)* Nym! It's me. I'm drunk, I forgot my key. Nym! Open up! You work for me so you've got to do what I say. Come on! It's me who doesn't pay the rent. *(Laughs.)* Nym!!

(MARX is gone. FAWKSEY coughing, moaning. NYM comes out of the stage right room and goes into the stage left room, closing the door behind her. FAWKSEY's coughing eases. MARX climbs in the sash window, collapses onto the floor. He stands, closes the window, then starts to walk around the flat but stubs his toe on a book. Enter NYM.)

MARX: Nym, why are my things strewn all over the floor?

NYM: Because the bailiffs didn't take the floor.

(MARX sinks down on the floor with his back to the wall.)

MARX: Foie gras?

(NYM goes into the kitchen and brings him a plate, the pâté.)

A knife?

(NYM looks at him.)

The bailiffs.

(MARX uses his fingers and spreads the pâté on the bread and eats voraciously.)

NYM: Give me a cigar.

MARX: I've only got the Polish fireworks.

NYM: I like those. I like the smell.

MARX: We have so much in common Nymchen.

(NYM lights the cigar skilfully. Puffs away and sits on the floor with her back to the wall.)

NYM: Where's the Argyll?

MARX: Where's the enemy?

NYM: I don't know where Jenny is.

MARX: Did she go with Willich?

NYM: You saw what I saw. That doesn't mean she's sleeping with him.

MARX: I'm sorry! You don't know how incredibly, existentially sorry I am.

NYM: Where's the Argyll?

MARX: If you take Jenny's side, in this I'll not have a friend left in the world.

NYM: I'm not going anywhere.

MARX: That is what I need. Unconditional love. In industrial quantities.

NYM: If you die tomorrow –

MARX: – why would I die tomorrow?

NYM: The duel.

MARX: Scheisse! Forgot about that. I get it! If I die tomorrow, no one knows where the Argyll is. I had to pawn it, we had no food for drink.

NYM: Money for drink.

MARX: Sorry, I've been drinking. Was ever a man, engaged in writing about the corrupting effects of money, so short of the bloody stuff.

NYM: Which pawnbroker's?! Mitchell's or Mr Fleece?

MARX: I'll tell you where the Argyll is if you tell me where my wife is?

NYM: That's childish.

MARX: Yes.

NYM: She's not here.

MARX: Mr Fleece.

NYM: Thank you.

MARX: I want a glass of wine.

NYM: Can I have one?

MARX: Nymchen, you're family, you don't have to ask.

NYM: It's not my wine.

MARX: Hell, it is your wine! All the nothing I've provided is yours!

(NYM pours two glasses of wine.)

On behalf of the Marx family, could I apologise. Most maidservants –

NYM: – I'm not a maid servant.

MARX: I didn't say you were, I said most maidservants. Most maidservants get a bed, time off, wages. Is it hell?

NYM: To be a maid in Salzwedel would be hell.

MARX: I hate that you are suffering because of me. That I have influenced you at all. I'm an idiot! Everything I say and do causes pain, suffering, and yes, yes –

NYM: – what?

MARX: Death. Thousands of good men, and, let's be fair, women have died. No one can accuse me of leaving the women out. I can't sleep. I can still see the flagstones red and wet with the blood of students, apprentices, young people Nym, dreamers! Their lives ended by a piece of shrapnel ripping through their livers. And they were there because they'd read the manifesto. I killed them. And I'm killing you, and Jenny, and Qui Qui and Fawksey. And when you die Nym, whatever death you have, early, late, painful, drawn out, miserable, cold, in a prison, that'll be me. Why don't these young people go out in the sun, and have picnics, and make love and drink at the well of their own serendipity, and stop thinking about the injustice and suffering of others. Live, laugh and bloody thrive! And they want the book in Russia. That's dangerous. The Russians are, you know, Russian. They eat pickled beetroot, and fuck their sisters. There's millions of them, we're not talking about Sussex. If I infect that lot with the virus of hope there will be perpetual conflict. What the hell right do I have to ask anyone to suffer a moment's inconvenience, never mind death. I want to be ignored!

NYM: But the truth cannot be ignored.

MARX: You want to know the truth. The enemy is pliable, elastic, shape shifting. Greed is the most powerful elixir of all. It inebriates reason and social justice. Purified and strengthened in the hands of an elite, it commands not just banks and the markets, but governments, whole states, who must underpin and serve it. Capitalism is a seven headed hydra that can't be killed.

NYM: The poor are suffering now.

MARX: Suffering? This life doesn't matter. You want meaning, go to church. All this? It's just a twelve line prologue. Compared to eternity, life's a fart. Kiss me.

NYM: Let me finish this cigar.

MARX: You wanted to tell me something earlier.

NYM: I can't tell you now.

MARX: We're alone.

NYM: You might die tomorrow.

MARX: You should marry. An attractive "not a maid servant" like you.

NYM: This is my life, and I like it. And it's not because I love you, although I do, it's because I know who I am. It is a rich and purposeful life and it is you who said –

MARX: – No! Please do not quote me to me!

NYM: "The chief guide which must direct us in our choice of profession is the welfare of mankind and our own perfection."

MARX: But Nymchen you are perfect. Kiss me.

NYM: Don't call me Nymchen, you know what happened the last time.

MARX: Nymlein. Kiss me.

(NYM kisses him, passionately, and then stops him.)

Jenny's not here.

NYM: She's not on a tour of Europe like last time.

MARX: I might take a bullet tomorrow.

NYM: Don't play that card, it's contemptible.

MARX: I know, I'm ashamed, but you know, come on Nym. I might take a bullet tomorrow.

(She kisses him, he responds, they fall into a deep embrace on the floor.)

End of Scene.

SCENE EIGHT

(On the way to Hampstead Heath. WILLICH, and BARTHÉLEMY.)

BARTHÉLEMY: Mon brave, 'ave you 'ad Marx's wife in your rooms?

WILLICH: I love her, she doesn't love me.

BARTHÉLEMY: *(Stops dead in his tracks.)* You took her to your rooms?! Go back and 'ave her now, in your rooms!

WILLICH: She doesn't love me.

BARTHÉLEMY: I do not wish to be the, 'ow you say deuxieme?

WILLICH: – second.

BARTHÉLEMY: – the second to a man who 'as 'ad a beautiful woman in your rooms and 'as not 'ad her, one time, two time, three time, and 'ow you say quatre –

WILLICH: – four.

BARTHÉLEMY: Four time. If you 'ave, in your rooms, une noisette d'agneau?

WILLICH: Noisette of lamb.

BARTHÉLEMY: Cuit à point, do you let it sleep, non, you eat it!

WILLICH: Frau Marx is not a lamb chop. Now come on! The sun will not wait. I will kill Marx.

BARTHÉLEMY: You do not 'ave to kill Marx to 'ave his wife, she is in your rooms.

WILLICH: The duel is about honour, not about Jenny Von Westphalen.

BARTHÉLEMY: D'accord! Kill Marx, but then, for me, and for God, go back and 'ave her in your rooms.

WILLICH: She doesn't love me.

BARTHÉLEMY: In France that doesn't matter, she is in your rooms, and you are a man, so you 'ave to 'ave her.

End of Scene.

SCENE NINE

(The heath. Doc SCHMIDT is marking out the 'points' for the duel. WILLICH, BARTHÉLEMY, ENGELS and MARX arrive.)

SCHMIDT: Gentlemen!

BARTHÉLEMY: Bonjour! You 'ave arrived.

WILLICH: You look tired Marx.

MARX: Au contraire, I slept like a log.

WILLICH: When I slay you, you will sleep to the end of eternity.

MARX: I have no wish to die a pedant, but eternity has no end, that's the unique and indeed defining quality of the concept of eternity.

ENGELS: Monsieur. It is the role of the seconds to explore an honourable resolution of the dispute.

WILLICH: I have been called one – an idiot; two – a fool; and three a priapic Prussian prick.

MARX: If you're struggling with the maths, put your hand up!

ENGELS: A retraction can be made respectfully.

WILLICH: I have no quarrel with you Engels.

ENGELS: Nor I with you. Comrades! Marx has simply confused friends and enemies, and for that he wishes to apologise.

WILLICH: From his mouth. The apology and retraction must come from his mouth, in supplication to me.

MARX: Where's my wife?

BARTHÉLEMY: She is in his rooms.

MARX: Is this true?

WILLICH: Yes, your wife is where she belongs.

MARX: *(Roars.)* You monstrous, moronic, cheating –

(MARX charges towards WILLICH. BARTHÉLEMY fells ENGELS with a vicious head butt.)

MARX: I'll rip your throat out!

(DOC SCHMIDT throws restraining arms around MARX.)

SCHMIDT: Restrain yourself comrade.

WILLICH: I'll kill him with my bare hands if I have to.

BARTHÉLEMY: I will bite him!

SCHMIDT: Herr Willich, no!

(Out of the mists, SCHRAMM arrives and hurries to MARX. They comfort ENGELS.)

We came as gentlemen, and we will fight as gentlemen.

MARX: Hand me a pistol!

(SCHMIDT hands pistols to ENGELS and BARTHÉLEMY.)

SCHMIDT: Gentlemen, to your points.

(MARX and the injured ENGELS, and WILLICH and BARTHÉLEMY walk to the points.)

Seconds prepare the weapons for those who duel. On my command you will turn, and I will say ready, aim and fire.

SCHRAMM: Herr Marx!

MARX: What is it Schramm?

SCHRAMM: I am here sir, we are here sir.

MARX: Who are we!?

SCHRAMM: We, the editorial board of the New New Rheinische Zeitung.

MARX: You've got a nose for a good story.

SCHRAMM: The second of March 1849 sir.

MARX: What?!

SCHRAMM: A date etched on the heart of every revolutionary émigré who has ever put pen to paper, thought into word, word into voice, in the cause of the overthrow of repressive regimes.

SCHMIDT: Turn gentlemen.

SCHRAMM: Prussian soldiers came to your house Herr Doktor Marx to arrest the writer Ernst Brauder but you would not let them pass. You held the threshold of your home and repelled the power of the state.

MARX: Schramm, you're in the firing line.

SCHRAMM: You are the revolution sir, its intellect, its spirit, its essence.

SCHMIDT: Raise your pistols!

SCHRAMM: The writers of the New New Rheinische Zeitung have come to save you sir.

(MARX pushes SCHRAMM to the ground.)

ENGELS: You're a damn fool Schramm! Get out the way!

SCHMIDT: Aim gentlemen.

(MARX and WILLICH take aim. SCHRAMM struggles to his feet and wrestles the pistol from MARX who tries to wrestle it back. SCHRAMM throws MARX to the ground and aims the pistol at WILLICH.)

SCHRAMM: I am but one man. It is an honour.

SCHMIDT: Fire!

(Two shots ring out. WILLICH and SCHRAMM remain standing for a couple of beats, and then SCHRAMM touches his head.)

SCHRAMM: Sweet mercy.

(SCHRAMM falls to his knees. DOC SCHMIDT attends him. A peeler's whistle, and two POLICE appear, everyone else runs. SCHRAMM keels over.)

Interval.

Act Two

SCENE ONE

(The flat. The morning of the duel. NYM, in a night shift, enters from the women's bedroom sobbing. Enter QUI QUI from the same room, also in a night dress.)

QUI QUI: Is my father dead?

NYM: No.

QUI QUI: Then why are you crying?

NYM: I'm allergic to a lack of furniture. The General would never let a duel happen. Come on! School!

QUI QUI: Is Mama with Herr Willich?

(NYM starts brushing QUI QUI's hair.)

NYM: No, no. What a tangle! Look! An owl's nest!

QUI QUI: Will I go to prison?

NYM: For what?

QUI QUI: We're his children. We're terrorists.

NYM: It is not a crime to be his child.

QUI QUI: Without Daddy, how will we live?

NYM: By breathing.

(There is a noise on the stairs.)

ENGELS: *(Off.)* To me! To you!

(QUI QUI unbolts the door, and in comes ENGELS and MARX pulling a piano, on top of which is a table and chairs. QUI QUI throws herself into MARX's arms.)

QUI QUI: Dadda!

ENGELS: Aargh! Do you know this incredibly expensive piano is resting on my foot?

MARX: You hum it and I'll play it. Marx and Engels!

ENGELS: Engels and Marx!

MARX: Princess, for you, the finest piano in Austria. How it got to London I do not know.

ENGELS: I pushed it from Vienna.

(QUI QUI is still hanging on to MARX and now crying.)

MARX: Hey, stop this! Come on, your very own Bosendorfer, and next year, when you're a little older –

QUI QUI: – a year older.

MARX: We'll hold a soiree and invite lots of young Englishmen and when they hear you play that little Mozart sonata the richest and most handsome one will fall hopelessly in love with you and ask me if he can marry you, and take you away to his castle on the Isle of Dogs.

ENGELS: Isle of Wight.

QUI QUI: But I'll only be eleven!

MARX: Eleven years old, and still bumming off your parents!

(MARX picks up QUI QUI. She giggles and screams.)

NYM: Stop teasing! She thought you were dead!

(MARX sings to the tune of Beethoven's Ode to Joy, maybe at the piano. ENGELS joins in.)

MARX/ENGELS:
Hegel, Hess and Feuerbach are stupider than Fichte is,
In a competition you could not tell who the victor is.
Kant Kant Kant could rave and rant, but none of his ravings can detract
From the brilliant Marx and Engels, Europe's favourite double act.

ENGELS: I'll pay the carter, shall I? It's amazing how much ready cash one needs living with the Marxes.

(ENGELS exits to pay the carter. MARX puts QUI QUI down and she runs to the piano and starts playing. ENGELS returns.)

ENGELS: Now that you're not dead, saved indeed, might this be seen as a sign that you have a purpose? 'The Economic Shit'.

MARX: – No definite article!

ENGELS: "Economic Shit". What are the chances of you passing the economic stool, sit down, or stand up and write the damn thing!

(NYM hands MARX a pan.)

MARX: Breakfast! We need breakfast!

ENGELS: You are the emperor of procrastination!

(A knock at the door.)

NYM: Doc Schmidt.

(NYM opens the door. And DOC SCHMIDT enters carrying the lists.)

ENGELS: Doc? What news of Schramm?

MARX: Is he dead?

SCHMIDT: I can't say. They arrested me, and carried him away.

MARX: You don't look arrested.

SCHMIDT: I convinced them that I was taking my morning constitutional and not a party to events. But I do have bad news. Schapper has been arrested in Cologne. We have an informer in our midst.

MARX: Was Willich arrested with you?

SCHMIDT: Willich was not arrested, indeed he walked down the road with the police, chatting and laughing.

MARX: Willich is Judas?

SCHMIDT: Aristocracy, Prussian, Cologne, a military
background, and he knows your wife's brother.

MARX: Are you implicating my wife?

SCHMIDT: Is she here?

MARX: You are!

SCHMIDT: Someone has to speak out.

(JENNY's knock at the door.)

MARX: The spy, my wife.

(QUI QUI unbolts the door and JENNY enters. QUI QUI hugs her.)

QUI QUI: Mamma!

JENNY: Is Willich dead?

MARX: You ask about your lover before your husband?

JENNY: I can see you're alive.

ENGELS: Willich lives, unfortunately. The police turned up.
We all ran.

JENNY: How's my boy?

SCHMIDT: I didn't come here for Fawksey. Comrades.

(SCHMIDT leaves.)

NYM: Fawksey is restless.

JENNY: Temperature?

NYM: It was high, but it's come down.

MARX: Jenny? Do you have something to tell me?

JENNY: Yes. Change your shirt. You've had it on for three days
now.

MARX: Did you sleep with that Prussian flagpole of yours.

NYM: Qui Qui, come with me –

MARX: – no! She needs to know what her mother is.

JENNY: I'm here, am I not.

MARX: Your being here tells me nothing.

JENNY: *(To ENGELS.)* Did Schramm find you?

ENGELS: He was hit.

JENNY: Hit!?

ENGELS: In the head.

JENNY: You let that boy –

MARX: – she'd rather I was dead!

JENNY: He worshipped you, and you let him –

MARX: – he took the pistol off me! The boy's a fully paid up half-wit. There's more brains in a large saveloy.

JENNY: My God you can be heartless.

MARX: *(To ENGELS.)* The frozen waste that is my wife.

NYM: Qui Qui.

MARX: She's not stupid! Are you princess? Play your mother the funeral march, cheer her up.

QUI QUI: I know Fur Elise.

MARX: Perfect! A frivolous bagatelle!

(QUI QUI starts playing.)

JENNY: I liked Schramm.

NYM: He is dead then?

ENGELS: It looks that way.

MARX: Let's not mourn the death of dunces. Schramm is dead, and forgotten. But, every cloud, silver lining, the New New Rheinische Zeitung will have a new new editor!

JENNY: *(To ENGELS.)* Have you seen this side of him? It's ugly.

MARX: Isn't the truth always.

JENNY: He didn't go to his father's funeral.

MARX: Snitch!

ENGELS: *My* father is a philistine, Calvinist, Prussian, tit on a horse, *but* I'll still be there at his funeral.

MARX: Because you're a mawkish, cluttered –

ENGELS: – cluttered?

MARX: – cluttered with duty. Mawkish, cluttered, fox hunting, cotton lord with a cock like a carthorse.

JENNY: Moor!

MARX: Qui Qui! Play one of Mendelsohn's breakfast overtures. Nym! Lard!

(FAWKSEY cries out. JENNY goes into the bedroom closing the door behind her.)

NYM: *(Sotto.)* I need to speak with you. Alone.

MARX: General! We need bacon, black pudding.

ENGELS: You want me to go out and buy bacon so you can talk about something with Nym.

MARX: Yes.

ENGELS: I'm going. Nym it's a perfectly normal cock.

MARX: Qui Qui! Go to the shops and help the General –

ENGELS: – carry the bacon?

QUI QUI: What?

ENGELS: I'll buy you some sherbet.

(ENGELS and QUI QUI leave. NYM and MARX are alone.)

MARX: Alone. What is it?

NYM: I'm sorry but you'll –

(JENNY opens the bedroom door and comes out.)

JENNY: Where's the honey?

NYM: He's had it all.

(Shouting out the window.) General, we need honey!

(JENNY looks between NYM and MARX. Then goes back into the room.)

NYM: I'm pregnant.

MARX: You're pregnant?

NYM: Yes.

MARX: It was only last night.

NYM: Two months ago. Greenwich park. Remember.

MARX: And are you saying –

(JENNY opens the door to the bedroom.)

JENNY: Fawksey says he'll eat something. Save one for him.

(JENNY closes the door. MARX puts a pan on the stove and rakes the coals.)

MARX: It can't be anyone else?

NYM: No.

MARX: Are you sure?

NYM: I've never slept with anyone else.

MARX: How do you know that?

NYM: Because I would have had to have been there when it happened.

MARX: And you would have remembered something like that?

NYM: Yes.

(JENNY comes out of the kitchen with a cup of water.)

JENNY: Remembered something like what?

MARX: Nym says she's only ever been to Greenwich with us.

JENNY: I've never been to Greenwich.

MARX: But she exists outside of us. She could've gone to any number of exotic destinations that we wouldn't know about.

(JENNY has gone back into the bedroom.)

MARX: Alright. I'm the father, but are you sure you're the mother?

NYM: What will happen?

MARX: Here? You, me, Engels, Jenny, Fawksey, Qui Qui, and your baby?

NYM: Do I need to leave?

NYM: What are we going to do?

MARX: Two options. I can kill myself, or I could sit in a corner and rock like a Bedlamite.

(JENNY comes out, checks the pan, stokes the fire, puts on more coal.)

JENNY: Every time I open that door you two stop talking.

FAWKSEY: *(Off.)* Daddy! Daddy!

JENNY: I'm many things, but I'm not Daddy.

(MARX goes into the bedroom.)

NYM: Are you alright Jenny?

JENNY: I try not to think about it.

NYM: I was worried about you, last night.

JENNY: Thank you.

(QUI QUI knocks.)

Qui Qui.

(NYM opens the door. Enter ENGELS and QUI QUI with bacon and sherbet.)

ENGELS: Half a pound of streaky, with a hint of sherbet lemon.

MARX: Excellent! I loathe the English, but they do understand one thing, the best things in life are fried!

(JENNY enters. MARX starts the process of cooking a fried breakfast.)

JENNY: Sweets before breakfast!?

MARX: Leave her alone! Her father survived a duel. Princess pianoforte! Eggs! When I say "egg" you throw. Egg!

(QUI QUI throws an egg to MARX who cracks it and starts to cook. JENNY exits.)

MARX: Qui Qui, at breakfast, there's a fundamental difference in motivation between the chicken and the pig.

QUI QUI: What do you mean daddy?

MARX: Vis a vis breakfast – the chicken is reasonably motivated, involved, happy to be asked –

QUI QUI: – eggs.

MARX: Yes! But the pig is committed. Bacon, throw!

(QUI QUI laughs and throws her father the bacon.)

ENGELS: This all smells good. Thank you Mister Engels.

MARX: Thank you Mister Engels for the bacon.

ENGELS: And the table and chairs.

QUI QUI: And the piano.

ENGELS: That's all I need, a little love.

MARX: A little love? Ha! If uncle Freddy doesn't have a different woman every couple of days he'll explode.

QUI QUI: What do you do with them Uncle Freddy?

(Laughter.)

ENGELS: Tea. I like to have tea with different women, in the afternoons, because I need tea, and they like tea.

MARX: Or his cock falls off.

(JENNY comes in.)

JENNY: Qui Qui, it's a school day.

QUI QUI: But Mamma?!

(An unsteady FAWKSEY staggers out of his room.)

FAWKSEY: I'm hungry Daddy.

MARX: Cuddle with squeeze, or cuddle with tickle?

FAWKSEY: Squeeze, don't tickle.

(MARX cuddles FAWKSEY but tickles him. He giggles.)

No, no, don't tickle!

JENNY: Mind his breathing.

(MARX puts him down.)

ENGELS: I could eat a horse, but this is not France.

FAWKSEY: Do they eat horses in France?

ENGELS: Continental breakfast, croissant, two hooves and jam.

(QUI QUI laughs, then maternally takes FAWKSEY into her arms.)

MARX: Look at it, before us.

NYM: What?

MARX: Breakfast. Look at that egg.

JENNY: Another epiphany.

(MARX holds his plate in the air, showing them his fried egg.)

MARX: I don't know who laid this egg.

QUI QUI: Chickens lay eggs Daddy, not people.

MARX: You wait, capitalism'll soon have a manufactory
churning out eggs by the thousands.

MARX: My point is that in earlier times, in say the feudal era –

ENGELS: – in worse times then?

MARX: At least I knew who I was!

MARX: Before capitalism I could see my brother's hand in the
labour content of my breakfast.

MARX: This sausage was metonymic of the social relations
prevalent at that time.

ENGELS: This is good, but write it down.

MARX: A sausage could explain my life.

ENGELS: Your species' essence.

MARX: In its offal lies the explanation of who I am.

ENGELS: It maps your social relations.

MARX: And reminds me that I am connected to my fellow man. But then came capitalism and its trusty dog, the money commodity –

ENGELS: – woof, woof!

MARX: – which destroyed all social relations allowing no other point of contact other than cash.

ENGELS: But cash –

MARX: – unlike sausages.

ENGELS: Can't tell us who we are.

JENNY: Cash does allow one to live with some dignity.

MARX: It alienates me, utterly.

ENGELS: Alienates? Good word.

MARX: Money prevents me seeing the labour of my brother, and if I can't see his labour, I can't see his life! All relations are commodified. Capitalism will even commodify the bones of the saints, and render religion obsolete. Christmas will disappear into capitalism's foul, gaping maw, and will be sicked up again, utterly commodified.

FAWKSEY: I love Christmas!

MARX: In ten years' time Christmas will no longer be a day to celebrate Christ's birth, it will be a week-long festival of commodification, a whole week, and so universal and meaningless that even Rabbis'll be scoffing mince pies, and snogging under the mistletoe.

(There is a loud knocking at the door.)

JENNY: No.

(MARX is already in the cupboard. JENNY goes to the door.)

Who is it?

SCHRAMM: *(Off.)* It's me!

JENNY: Schramm!

(JENNY opens the door. SCHRAMM enters. Bandaged.)

Conrad!

(She holds him.)

SCHRAMM: Agh!

NYM: We thought you were dead!

ENGELS: Mon brave!

(ENGELS hugs SCHRAMM. SCHRAMM approaches the cupboard.)

SCHRAMM: Herr Doktor Marx! I am dead and then reborn, like Dionysus son of Zeus, I am torn to pieces and eaten by Titans, but I have faced down Thanatos, and Rhea has brought me back to life to live, write, talk, digress and go on and on for ever! Serendipity, the gods, fortune –

MARX: *(From the cupboard.)* Tautology, tautology, tautology! He's bloody worse than ever!

(ENGELS opens the cupboard door and pulls MARX out.)

ENGELS: Come on, give him a kiss.

MARX: You selfish bastard!

SCHRAMM: I am alive!

MARX: Why?!

SCHRAMM: Fate!

MARX: Sweet Mercy!

(SCHRAMM lustily embraces MARX.)

SCHRAMM: Your wit sir, I am overjoyed to find, is mercifully undiminished by your ordeal.

MARX: Why aren't you dead?

SCHRAMM: The bullet only grazed my temple.

MARX: *(To ENGELS.)* You told me Willich was a crack shot?

SCHRAMM: His aim, I confess myself modestly grateful to report, on this singular occasion, fell somewhat below his customary standard of deadly perfection.

MARX: Maybe, but I've lined up a new new editor for the Zeitung.

SCHRAMM: *(Laughs.)* If I may pick up on the elegant coat tails of your epigram, might I perhaps presume to apologise profusely for not being dead.

MARX: Apology not accepted.

SCHRAMM: I am bested in wit once again by a master of that specialised craft.

MARX: *(To ENGELS.)* You piss in his face and he thanks you for the baptism.

JENNY: I was beside myself with worry.

SCHRAMM: Madam Marx, you do me, by a very considerable degree, too great a kindness.

JENNY: Have you eaten?

MARX: No!

SCHRAMM: I would not presume to impose upon your generous hospitality, but no I haven't, thank you.

(He sits and picks up a knife and fork.)

MARX: You have the impertinence not to die, and then you eat my breakfast. I shall be in the reading room of the British Museum if you wish to send a written apology. Do not deliver it yourself!

(MARX leaves.)

ENGELS: He's working! He's gone to work. He's writing. Finally. Schramm you are a genius!

(ENGELS kisses SCHRAMM on the forehead.)

End of Scene.

TRANSITION

(In the street. MARX walking along, he realises that HELMUT is following him. MARX stops, HELMUT stops.)

MARX: Helmut. Why are you following me?

HELMUT: Because the Prussian Minister of the Interior pays me well.

MARX: But you know where I'm going.

HELMUT: I'd guess the British Museum Reading Room where you will read a very big, very heavy, difficult book, standing up, on account of your boils.

MARX: You told them about my boils?

HELMUT: Couple of sentences in the report, yeah. They like detail.

MARX: Who is betraying me?

HELMUT: I can't tell you, that'd be silly.

MARX: Willich? Is it Willich? Engels? Nym? Jenny? Doc Schmidt? Conrad Schramm?

(HELMUT coughs.)

Conrad?!

HELMUT: No. I just coughed.

MARX: But he took a bullet for me, it can't be Conrad.

HELMUT: I have a cold. *(HELMUT blows his nose.)*

And excuse me, I'm going to sneeze.

(MARX runs off. HELMUT sneezes.)

MARX: *(Off.)* Gesundheit!

HELMUT: Doktor Marx! Why do you insist on making my life difficult!?

SCENE TWO

(The Reading Room of the British Museum. A man of about sixty sits reading/writing upstage centre of a large study table. Behind him there are three other smaller study tables, each has a male 'reader' with their head down in books or specimens. The sixty year old looks exactly like the iconic figure of MARX we know from the headstone. MARX walks in and sees him, double takes, turns and stands at a table (he can't sit because of the boils) but can't help being impressed by the bearded figure. The man catchs MARX looking at him. They both work. MARX looks up at him. The man looks up, and catches MARX looking at him.)

BEARDED MAN: Can I help?

MARX: Do I know you?

BEARDED MAN: Are you interested in barnacles?

MARX: As in *stuck to a ship* barnacles?

BEARDED MAN: Yes.

MARX: Nie. I have never been diverted from my life's purpose mit barnacles.

BEARDED MAN: Then you're a fool. Because you are a barnacle.

MARX: Absolutely foolish, yes, aber a barnacle?

BEARDED MAN: We're all barnacles.

MARX: Metaphorically?

BEARDED MAN: Literally. Are you not driven to understand who you are? I'm talking about the foundations of life, of –

MARX: – the origin of the species?

BEARDED MAN: *(Beat.)* That's good. Can I have that?

MARX: Ich habe no use for it.

(The BEARDED MAN writes something down.)

Do the barnacle und man share eine mutter?

BEARDED MAN: The barnacles took the low road, we took the high the road.

MARX: Also, Ich bin ein barnacle! Every day ist ein school day.

LIBRARIAN: Shh!

(Enter ENGELS.)

ENGELS: Moor!?

READER 1: Shh!

MARX: Yes.

READER 2: Shh!

ENGELS: Where?

READER 1: Shh!

MARX: Here.

READER 2: Shh!

ENGELS: Crisis. News from Cologne.

MARX: From where?

READER 2: Cologne.

ENGELS: Shh! The committee are arrested.

MARX: Moll?

ENGELS: Moll, Anneke, the whole committee!

(A READER stands and exits leaving his book/samples on the desk.)

MARX: After Schapper, we knew that would happen. I have a domestic problem.

ENGELS: – the entire central committee are in prison!

MARX: And Nym has got a bun in the oven. And I'm the baker.

ENGELS: You fucked the maid?!!

ALL: Shush!!!!!!

LIBRARIAN: I cannot endorse this! Leave. Now!

MARX: I'm really incredibly sorry Mrs Whitehead.

ENGELS: I apologise.

(LIBRARIAN walks away.)

You fucked the maid!!!

(Everyone looks up again. One READER picks up his books and leaves in disgust.)

Sorry!

MARX: You know what this means?

ENGELS: Nine months' gestation and then a baby?

MARX: Mon brave, you're going to have to take responsibility.

ENGELS: For what?

MARX: I need you to say you're the father.

ENGELS: You want everyone to think that I fucked the maid!?

READER: Shh!

ENGELS: You shush!

MARX: For my marriage, for Jenny, for the movement.

ENGELS: Are you insane?!

MARX: My enemies will destroy me with this. My reputation –

ENGELS: – what of my reputation?

MARX: You do not have a reputation to defend. Fucking maids is your metier.

READER: Woah!

ENGELS: Never!

(ENGELS stands suddenly, kicking a chair over which causes a chain reaction domino style of destruction which causes other readers to protect their books and specimens. MRS WHITEHEAD returns with a man in a beige work coat.)

ENGELS: You arrogant, selfish, bastard!

LIBRARIAN: That's enough, out, both of you!

(The librarian's assistant grabs ENGELS. ENGELS nuts him. A reader punches ENGELS, MARX punches the reader that punched ENGELS, another reader rugby tackles ENGELS onto the big table, samples go all over, a bookcase goes over followed by screams and the other readers join in Wild West style, using large books like chairs in a saloon brawl to smash each other over the heads. Think Alan Ladd in Shane. ENGELS is dragged off.)

ENGELS: I will never agree to this!

BEARDED MAN: Mrs Whitehead? Has the Reverend Klinkard finished with DeLacy's *Almanack of Molluscs*?

LIBRARIAN: When I get a moment, I'll go and look.

BEARDED MAN: Thank you.

End of Scene.

SCENE THREE

(The Dean Street flat. MARX, ENGELS and NYM. MARX and ENGELS are both sporting bandages.)

NYM: A fight in a library?

MARX: It was a typical library brawl. Somebody threw a punch at my friend, so, as you do, I went in.

NYM: But you wanted to talk to me?

MARX: The thing is…and it is not entirely straightforward, this thing, but it is a thing that can be managed, wonderfully successfully in fact, with other things being part of it. And those things will fall into place as things happen, making the thing itself a more than passable thing.

NYM: My baby.

MARX: Is the thing we are talking about.

ENGELS: You bastard.

NYM: *(To ENGELS.)* You know?

MARX: He knows.

NYM: I never wanted to cause pain between you and Jenny.

MARX: No, no, yes, no, I understand –

NYM: I love Jenny like a sister, but I cannot deny my feelings. Is that wrong?

MARX: It's a valid question, full of validity, and I'm glad you –

NYM: – my love is not illegitimate –

ENGELS: – unlike the baby.

MARX: You must have the child.

NYM: Our child!

MARX: General here has agreed, with unselfish altruism, to be the, um, you know, to the, er child.

NYM: Godfather! Thank you.

ENGELS: You bastard.

MARX: The father.

NYM: What?

MARX: He's always quite liked you.

ENGELS: You absolute bastard.

MARX: This might not be exactly what you had in mind Nym.

NYM: What extraordinary insight into womankind you have.

MARX: Are my political enemies to be given the gift of my social ignominy?

NYM: Is that what our child means to you? Social ignominy?

MARX: Ignominy, scandal, humiliation, let's not split hairs! The movement, the revolution, these are our true children.

ENGELS: I just threw up a bit in my mouth.

MARX: The child will officially be the General's. He will make provision for the foster parents, and we'll find good people.

NYM: You bastard.

MARX: I'm married! The public revelation of a child born out of wedlock would ruin me.

ENGELS: You absolute bastard.

NYM: But no one will believe that the General is father to my child?

MARX: They will! You have been seduced by the great seducer!

(ENGELS grabs him by the lapels.)

ENGELS: Du bist wirklich ein total dreck-kotzgefullter-hosenscheisse-arschklarsch-wanzsphilitische-Feigling!

MARX: That's all agreed then.

(JENNY's knock.)

MARX: Jenny! You two, into the bedroom.

(MARX ushers NYM and ENGELS into the bedroom. JENNY knocks.)

I'm coming!

(MARX lets her in.)

You're on your own?

JENNY: They're at the Gilberts'.

MARX: Qui Qui's friend's?

JENNY: Yes. Fawksey loves Mrs Gilbert, and she feeds them up.

MARX: But –

JENNY: – he's not coughing. I wouldn't have left them if –

MARX: – alright, I trust you.

(A look.)

Guess who's been round.

JENNY: Who?

MARX: The General.

JENNY: Where is he?

MARX: Do you need to ask?

JENNY: Are you going to tell me?

MARX: Do I really have to?

JENNY: Do you really want to?

MARX: He came round, like a love struck teenager, powered by a heady mixture of infatuation and anticipation.

NYM: *(Off.)* You're mad!

ENGELS: *(Off.)* I do not deny it!

JENNY: Mary Burns is here?

MARX: No, no, no. I hardly need to tell you the identity of the wholly reciprocating recipient of his amour?

NYM: *(Off.)* But this is so ridiculous! Did you volunteer!?

ENGELS: *(Off.)* He had me nailed to the wall, what else could I bloody do!?

(NYM has kicked or punched a cupboard door.)

MARX: Ooh! This one really does seem to be 'la grande passion'.

JENNY: Who has he got in there?

MARX: Nym.

JENNY: Nym? And him?

MARX: Him and Nym.

JENNY: He –

MARX: – and Ny. When you think about it it's obvious.

JENNY: No! It isn't. They don't particularly like each other.

MARX: I know, I was shocked, initially. I thought Nym with him, no. Maybe more him with Nym, to begin, but no, Nym was as into him and he into Ny.

JENNY: And they're?

MARX: In there. Took the opportunity, with the kids out the house. Couldn't stop them. Like two young lovebirds, or rabbits, or in season mink.

ENGELS: *(Off.)* Alright! I don't care anymore, hit me, go on, hit me!

NYM: *(Off.)* What makes you think you'll get away with this!?

ENGELS: *(Off.)* Put that down. No, don't!!

(Noise of something being thrown, and smashed, an actual breakage.)

MARX: Mmm. Lively. It's a little presumptious, in our place, but I guess we're all adults.

(Another smash.)

They're really good together.

(ENGELS and NYM enter about as far apart as is possible.)

You two, tch! Welcome back.

(NYM and ENGELS sit, separately.)

JENNY: Hello Nym.

NYM: Hello Jenny.

JENNY: Hello General.

ENGELS: Hello Jenny.

(Silence.)

MARX: This is nice. Drink? Bit early in the day, but I think I have some quite acceptable Scotch from a previous visit from the General.

JENNY: Moor was just saying –

MARX: – that, um, you two, both of you, were, as a couple, both together, and wasn't it a bit of a surprise, but also very lovely for both of the two of you lovely people to be together as a lovely couple.

JENNY: I had no idea.

(NYM and ENGELS can barely look at each other.)

MARX: It was obvious to me!

ENGELS: What?

JENNY: When did you two first…

MARX: – General? Ladies first I know, but Freddy? It was definitely more than eight weeks ago?

ENGELS: I'd say eight weeks and two days ago.

JENNY: And you felt the same Nym?

NYM: No.

MARX: What?!

NYM: My feelings went back further. I was attracted to a man I had admired for more than ten years.

JENNY: Oh sweet. And General, you found yourself feeling the same way?

ENGELS: Similar. Along those lines.

MARX: *(With glass.)* What more joyous than celebrating love between two people. What more? Unless there was something more, or additional, to celebrate on top of it. Or with it, or connected in some way, or as a result.

NYM: I'm pregnant.

MARX: Now I did not expect that!

JENNY: Nym!

(JENNY embraces NYM.)

MARX: This is wonderful news indeed.

(ENGELS downs his second large whisky in one, and pours himself another.)

JENNY: Nymchen!? How are you feeling?

NYM: Terrible.

(JENNY holds her closer.)

ENGELS: Me too.

JENNY: *(To NYM.)* Morning sickness?

ENGELS: Yes.

MARX: Sympathetic pains. A true mark of love.

JENNY: How long now?

NYM: Eight weeks.

JENNY: And two days?

NYM: *(Crying.)*

JENNY: Don't cry. This is happy news.

NYM: Yes, I am very happy.

ENGELS: We both are.

NYM: I'd like to lie down.

JENNY: Yes. Come to the bedroom.

(JENNY takes NYM to the bedroom. MARX pours another drink.)

ENGELS: Happy, Daddy?

MARX: Thanks a lot. I mean you really entered into the spirit of that.

ENGELS: You bastard.

MARX: You know, there's a really cynical side to you.

(JENNY comes back out of the bedroom.)

JENNY: She's completely wrung out. The emotion. But she's settled now.

MARX: Some women would have been pretty annoyed their maid had become pregnant. But not this woman General. Wife, mother – not my mother – secretary, amanuensis.

(JENNY knees MARX hard in the balls.)

I can explain.

JENNY: I am disappointed in you General.

(ENGELS protects his groin.)

ENGELS: I am disappointed in myself!

(Loud banging on the front door.)

SGT SAVAGE: Police! Unlock the door!

(MARX walks on his knees into the cupboard. JENNY opens the front door.)

SGT SAVAGE: Ah yes, I thought I'd been here already. Mister Engels.

ENGELS: It's good to see you again Sergeant.

SGT SAVAGE: Where is he? Charles Marx.

ENGELS: Jenny hasst du –

JENNY: Jawohl!

(JENNY opens the cupboard door.)

SGT SAVAGE: Mister Marx?

MARX: Is it illegal in England to have relations outside of marriage?

SGT SAVAGE: Mr. Charles Marx…I never know what to say in this situation….I've come to inform you, as a suspected felon, of a reported act involving a piece of silverware, what has gone missing from its rightful possessor, and as a corollary I am empowered to place your person in custody.

MARX: You're arresting me on suspicion of the theft of an Argyll?

SGT SAVAGE: Brilliant. I'll make a note of that wording.

MARX: Das Argyll ist a family heirloom. Ein wedding present. Ergo, it is mine und hers!

SGT SAVAGE: Is this true madam?

JENNY: Mein Argyll ist missing. Und I don't know this man.

(The OFFICER cuffs MARX.)

MARX: Jenny!

(The OFFICER takes him away.)

End of Scene.

SCENE FOUR

(MARX is at the cell door in discussion with a sceptical gaoler who is reading to him.)

SINGE: *(Reading.)* "Hegel's argument is essentially mystical and idealistic, whereas my dialectic is the antithesis, rooted in a materialistic view of man's situation. So, as a man, without economic autonomy, utterly alienated from my brother worker, and suffering grinding poverty, I decided to nick a solid silver gravy warmer."

MARX: I'm happy mit that.

SINGE: Sign here. And date it please. The Beak'll have fun with that.

(SINGE passes the statement through the bars and MARX signs it. A door is heard opening, off. Enter CONSTABLE CRIMP with WILLICH and BARTHÉLEMY.)

SINGE: What are these two in for?

CONSTABLE CRIMP: Duelling. Yesterday morning. On the heath. Arrested at Charing Cross today, trying to leg it.

BARTHÉLEMY: Je suis Francais!

CONSTABLE CRIMP: Eh?

WILLICH: I am French.

CONSTABLE CRIMP: *(To WILLICH.)* You're French?

WILLICH: No.

CONSTABLE CRIMP: Don't lie to the police then son.

WILLICH: He's French.

CONSTABLE CRIMP: *(To BART.)* Good, you'll be impressed by the plumbing.

(CRIMP thrusts a bucket into BARTHÉLEMY's hands.)

MARX: August Willich, is that you?

WILLICH: Marx? What are you doing here?

MARX: Discussing dialectical materialism with Constable Singe.

WILLICH: I am arrested.

MARX: I don't believe a word of it.

SINGE: Cell eleven at the end.

CONSTABLE CRIMP: Right, come on lads, follow me.

BARTHELEMEY: Eleven?

WILLICH: Onze.

MARX: You can count to eleven Willich, I've seen you do it. Five fingers on each hand makes ten, and then you get your cock out.

WILLICH: Why do you not believe my word, that I am arrested?

MARX: Because Schapper is custody in Cologne! And you –

WILLICH: – you think I am the informer?! You do not know yourself Marx! You want, you need your rival in love to be your Judas. Life would be simpler that way, but unfortunately for you, I am a man of honour, true to our cause, *and* I am arrested!

BARTHÉLEMY: Moi aussi!

MARX: Doc Schmidt told me you –

WILLICH: – Schmidt!? You never see the lies you believe!

(Enter ENGELS led by SGT SAVAGE.)

SGT SAVAGE: Miladdo's bailed.

CONSTABLE CRIMP: That's it! I've had enough of this babble! Chop, chop! Come on, this way.

(CRIMP takes them to the cells.)

SINGE: Rich friends eh?

(SINGE unlocks the cell and opens the gate.)

MARX: How did you arrange bail?

ENGELS: Circumstances.

MARX: Circumstances?

ENGELS: Fawksey.

MARX: What's happened?

ENGELS: He's gone. I'm sorry.

MARX: What 'gone'? Gone? No, not 'gone'.

ENGELS: He didn't wake this morning. He died during the night.

(MARX falls to his knees.)

MARX: No, no, no.

SINGE: I will pray for him.

ENGELS: Thank you.

SINGE: You're free to go Mister Marx.

(SINGE leaves.)

(MARX moans quietly and holds his own head in his hands. Then he comes out of it, quickly.)

MARX: Was Doc Schmidt there when Fawksey died?

ENGELS: No.

MARX: You remember when we nicked the gate?

ENGELS: Moor?! Fawksey is dead.

MARX: Doc Schmidt was with us, wasn't he?

ENGELS: What –

MARX: – He asked about the Argyll.

ENGELS: What are you talking about?!

MARX: And at the duel he attended Schramm and was not arrested. It's Doc Schmidt!

(MARX is on his feet and out of the cell.)

ENGELS: *(Grabs him.)* Jenny needs you!

MARX: Fawksey's dead. He is, as you said, gone. I cannot bring him back and I will not look back. In my position, in the vanguard of our greater cause, there is an imperative not to allow emotions and human frailty to suck away at my application.

ENGELS: But you must bury your son!

MARX: I will not take a lecture in family from you.

ENGELS: If you don't go to your own child's funeral, really, I don't know what species of beast I've been calling a friend.

MARX: Chacun à son goût General.

ENGELS: I'm finished with you! You've strayed far beyond the privilege of genius.

End of Scene.

SCENE FIVE

(Berwick street. MARX enters, sits on a step and waits. A door opens and DOC SCHMIDT exits carrying a suitcase, wearing a hat and great coat.)

MARX: Give it back Schmidt.

SCHMIDT: Moor, good to see you.

MARX: Give it back!

SCHMIDT: You have me at a disadvantage –

MARX: – I should kill you.

SCHMIDT: Kill me later! Let's have a whisky –

MARX: Give me the Argyll.

SCHMIDT: Even if I have what you say I have, which I don't admit, I have to return it to its rightful owner.

MARX: Fawksey's dead.

SCHMIDT: I'm sorry.

MARX: Are you?

SCHMIDT: I am a doctor. I treated his symptoms, correctly, with borax administered with honey. It wasn't me that killed him.

(MARX runs at SCHMIDT, knocks him down, pins him to the ground.)

MARX: *(To SCHMIDT.)* You were a friend.

SCHMIDT: I serve Prussia.

(SCHMIDT fumbles inside his greatcoat and produces the Argyll. MARX takes it.)

MARX: Who controls you? Jenny's brother?

SCHMIDT: Minister Von Westphalen's sent me to break the League and recover the family silver.

MARX: And destroying my marriage!?

SCHMIDT: You've got the Argyll, let me go.

(MARX raises his arm again, poised to bring the cobble down on SCHMIDT's head.)

MARX: You killed Fawksey!

SCHMIDT: You can't do it Marx, you're not a soldier.

(MARX pauses, then brings the stone down hard on SCHMIDT's head. The bystanders wade in and break them up.)

End of Scene.

SCENE SIX

(A graveyard and a hole in the ground, with fresh earth around. A gravedigger sits smoking a pipe. Enter a procession made up of a Lutheran PASTOR, JENNY and ENGELS carrying a small wooden coffin. QUI QUI, then NYM. They put the box by the hole. JENNY looks around.)

PASTOR: Frau Marx?

(JENNY ignores him.)

We're half an hour over and I have a baptism at –

JENNY: Mein Mann ist noch nicht da!

PASTOR: But –

ENGELS: – Pastor Flint, please, may we just wait another minute?

(The PASTOR stands five yards away. QUI QUI sits on a bench away from the grave.)

NYM: He'll come.

JENNY: You don't know him. He considers the dead lucky.

(NYM takes this as some kind of rebuke, and slopes off to sit on the bench with QUI QUI.)

ENGELS: His own son's funeral!

JENNY: He doesn't do funerals. He won't even go to his own.

PASTOR: Ma'am.

JENNY: Ja, was den? *(Yes, what?)*

PASTOR: We really need to begin.

JENNY: Ja, I apologise, it appears that mein Mann is indisposed.

(JENNY, ENGELS, and the PASTOR, with the help of the gravedigger lower the coffin into the ground. QUI QUI and NYM step forward. They all throw some soil in.)

PASTOR: You may speak to the child before I give the dedication.

ENGELS: Do you want me to say something?

89

JENNY: I'll try.

(Beat. And then JENNY speaks.)

Born on Guy Fawkes night 1847 my son Guido Fawksey Marx, I shall live your life for you so that you suffer no more bronchitis, measles, the croup, the colic –

(She starts to cry. ENGELS comforts her. SCHRAMM enters.)

SCHRAMM: Frau Doktor Marx –

ENGELS: – not now Schramm.

(ENGELS marshalls SCHRAMM away from the grave.)

JENNY: What –

SCHRAMM: – I wished to pay my respects to one who knew too little of the world, one robbed by untimely time of his place at life's feast –

ENGELS: – Schramm?!

SCHRAMM: Yes, sir. I know sir that I am prone to prolixity. My life has become a quest for brevity.

ENGELS: This is a child's funeral!

SCHRAMM: So I will convey my secondary purpose in attending upon this ceremony with uncharacteristic economy.

ENGELS: What's happened?!

SCHRAMM: Herr Doctor Marx has curtailed the egregious and nefarious machinations of a traitor.

PASTOR: Frau Marx, please, I must complete the service.

JENNY: Yes, yes.

SCHRAMM: Doc Schmidt is the informer! Herr Doktor Marx wounded the cur, and it was whilst the dog was in hospital that we found about his person plans to arrest a further twenty comrades across Europe. They have been forewarned! And that is why Doctor Marx is not here!

(Enter MARX.)

MARX: *(To the PASTOR.)* Who are you?

ENGELS: This is Pastor Flint, who is to give the dedication.

MARX: Und you, did you dig diese grave?

GRAVE DIGGER: Aye, sir.

MARX: Danke. Und a fine grave it is.

(MARX hugs him.)

Join us.

GRAVE DIGGER: Sir?

MARX: No man should be ashamed of his working clothes.

(The GRAVE DIGGER stays.)

PASTOR: We give thanks to God for the deceased, and commend the remains to God's care. Nothing can separate us from the love of God in Christ Jesus our Lord, not even death, and –

MARX: – enough! My son doesn't need your stories. The only truth here is our pain. Please, leave us with that. Jenny, have you spoken?

JENNY: Yes, I tried.

ENGELS: But he needs to hear your voice.

MARX: Yes. *(Beat.)* Fawksey! Son! I'm here. It's your father. Late, yes, but you knew I'd be late. And for that, I ask for your forgiveness. You were my son and an Englishman, and we bury you today in the soil of your mother country, and you take your rightful place with their great men. Wat Tyler, Henry Hunt, Thomas Paine, Oliver Cromwell, and William Shakespeare.

(To the GRAVEDIGGER.) Comrade, deine Schaufel please?

(The GRAVEDIGGER gives him his spade.)

I should've dug your grave, as a penance, punishment for the pain I caused you, but that would've been easy, and selfish. I'll fill it in, and this labour, is the gift I give you.

(He fills in the grave, and gives the spade back to the GRAVEDIGGER.)

Thank you brother.

MARX: General?

ENGELS: Qui Qui, come with me.

(MARX and JENNY are left alone.)

MARX: I killed him.

JENNY: Stop it.

MARX: Poor little mite. He never had a chance. Innocent, dragged into this. If I'd –

JENNY: – stop it!

MARX: I could've got a job on –

JENNY: – the railway?

MARX: Yes! Why not?

JENNY: That was never an option.

MARX: It's good enough for everyone else. And those people, they don't sacrifice their children.

JENNY: Everything we've ever done, we've done together.

MARX: We haven't done anything yet. *(Beat.)* Do you forgive me? For me and Nym.

JENNY: No.

MARX: Good. That's good. It's clear. We know where we are on that one. *(Beat.)* I forgive you.

JENNY: For what?

MARX: You're right. I'm sorry. You haven't done anything have you. I don't forgive you.

JENNY: Moor, don't make me laugh.

MARX: Sorry.

(He reaches out and takes her hand.)

MARX: Fawksey? What can we do? Me and your mother. To honour you. Carry on?

End of Scene.

SCENE SEVEN

(The flat. Seven months later. Evening. MARX is stood writing. JENNY is sat to one side transcribing MARX's scribble into legible handwriting. ENGELS has a glass of wine and alternates between tending the fire, and reading. NYM is organising filing cards. QUI QUI is playing the piano, sotto. The Argyll is there on JENNY's table.)

JENNY: *(With papers in hand.)* General?

ENGELS: That's me, I'm still here. For which I apologise.

MARX: Stay for dinner. You're family.

JENNY: We love you.

ENGELS: Nym?

NYM: I didn't say anything.

(They laugh. ENGELS pours wine for NYM.)

ENGELS: Have some more wine.

JENNY: *(With papers in hand.)* – what –

MARX: – You put the wine in the gravy warmer?!

ENGELS: Someone had to find a use for it.

(NYM drinks it without thanking or looking at ENGELS. ENGELS taps his glass with a fork or similar.)

JENNY: An official announcement.

ENGELS: I've decided to abandon you. I'm going back to Manchester.

NYM: Hurrah!

(They laugh.)

MARX: You hate Manchester.

ENGELS: I wrote to my father.

MARX: 'Please can I have my job back?'

JENNY: But you've just got rooms in Soho.

MARX: You're properly going to be a cotton lord?

ENGELS: I will send you a five pound note every week.

JENNY: And where will you get this five pound note?

ENGELS: I'll shall steal it from the cash box at Ermen and
Engels, risking dismissal by either Ermen or Engels.

NYM: You're Engels.

ENGELS: Which is why I might get away with it. And I will do
this partly because I believe his writing will contribute to
the progress of mankind, but more importantly because
there is another soul out there more in need of the job of
railway clerk at Paddington.

(MARX stands and embraces him.)

MARX: Marx and Engels.

ENGELS: Engels and Marx.

MARX: Thank you Freddy.

ENGELS: Now, I'm sorry Jenny, you wanted to ask me a question.

JENNY: Yes. As a cotton lord yourself –

NYM: Capitalist.

JENNY: *(Reading.)* Capital is dead labour, that vampire-like,
only lives by sucking living labour –

MARX: – and lives the more, the more labour it sucks.

ENGELS: This is meant to be a book about political economy,
not a penny dreadful. And two sucks in one sentence.

JENNY: One sucking, and one suck.

ENGELS: It's a bit bloody bloodthirsty.

NYM: It's an accurate metaphor. The capitalist is vampiric, a
blood sucker.

MARX: You pay the worker a shilling, but he creates three
shillings' of value.

NYM: You've vampire sucked two shillings surplus value.

MARX: Labour is different from other commodities, it has the
capacity to create a value greater than its own value.

ENGELS: That's the only reason to buy it!

MARX: That is where capitalism is anti-thetical to natural
justice!

ENGELS: The capitalist pays a shilling for something he knows
to be worth three shillings.

JENNY: And you give no share in the surplus created.

NYM: You're a vampire.

ENGELS: I don't start til Monday.

JENNY: But why does the worker agree to this unjust exchange?

ENGELS: He has to eat.

JENNY: And pay the rent.

MARX: No!

NYM: Because there's someone who will work for less.

MARX: Thank you Nym. Surplus value is the modern battle
ground. Collective capital versus collective labour. This
battle will write the history of man in the next century.
Where's my wine then?

ENGELS: Is he allowed to drink and bring down capitalism at
the same time?

MARX: Yes!

MARX: L'chaim!

ENGELS: Zum Wohl! *(To health!)*

(They drink. ENGELS pours MARX a glass and looks over his shoulder.)

ENGELS: Are we sticking with sucking vampires then?

MARX: Yes.

ENGELS: This isn't work!

MARX: Piss off.

ENGELS: He's hiding something Jenny.

MARX: A private letter.

ENGELS: There's nothing private in here. We're communists!

(QUI QUI stops playing and looks for a new piece of sheet music.)

QUI QUI: Chopin?

MARX: Polish!

QUI QUI: Liszt?

ENGELS: Hungarian!?

QUI QUI: Schumann?

ALL: German!

(QUI QUI looks for her sheet music and during the next she plays Kinderszenenen Op. 15, No. 1. ENGELS kisses JENNY on the forehead. A baby cries.)

NYM: Jenny? Would you like to go?

JENNY: May I? *(JENNY goes into the bedroom, and returns with the baby. She rocks the baby gently.)*

(ENGELS tends the fire. QUI QUI starts playing the Schumann again, and under. MARX finishes the letter and puts it down on the table next to JENNY.)

ENGELS: *(French.)* Attention! C'est fini! The secret letter thing.

MARX: *(To NYM.)* I'm sorry, I'd like Jenny to read a letter.

(NYM takes the baby. JENNY picks up the letter.)

MARX: Read it.

JENNY: Out loud?

MARX: Please.

(QUI QUI stops playing.)

JENNY: *(Reading.)* My dearest Jenny, I shall be martyred for my philosophy. Traduced, vilified, defamed. I care little, because that is not my life's work. My purpose on this earth, which is private, is to love you. There have been poets, braggards all, who, facetiously, have rhymed a greater love, but they were ignorant of my heart. Had they looked inside it, they would have deferred, stepped aside, and handed me the quill. Of course, I failed you. I looked away, to another. You took me back, and embraced her, without judgement, and without hesitation. That is why I shall always be unworthy of you. But if there is anything good and pure in me, it is yours, and can be found in my heart. Your loving husband, Moor.

(QUI QUI starts playing again.)

MARX: "It becomes the unique job of the money commodity –

NYM: – I don't like "unique job".

ENGELS: It's not a job is it?

NYM: Special social function.

ENGELS: How about I write Das Kapital and we just put your name on it?

MARX: "It becomes the special social function of the money commodity, and consequently its social monopoly, to play within the world of commodities the part of the general substitute"

JENNY: I don't like general substitute.

NYM: Universal exchange?

ENGELS: Universal substitute?

MARX: Universal equivalent. Money as the universal equivalent! Excellent. Thank you! Thank you. Thank you.

(QUI QUI plays on.)

THE END

WWW.OBERONBOOKS.COM